Unglued
Devotional

Also by Lysa TerKeurst

Becoming More Than a Good Bible Study Girl

Becoming More Than a Good Bible Study Girl video curriculum

Made to Crave

Made to Crave Devotional

Made to Crave video curriculum

Unglued

Unglued video curriculum

UNGLUED
Devotional

60 DAYS OF IMPERFECT PROGRESS

LYSA TERKEURST

NEW YORK TIMES BESTSELLING AUTHOR

ZONDERVAN.com/
AUTHORTRACKER
follow your favorite authors

ZONDERVAN

Unglued Devotional
Copyright © 2012 by Lysa TerKeurst

This title is also available as a Zondervan ebook. Visit www.zondervan.com/ebooks.

This title is also available in a Zondervan audio edition. Visit www.zondervan.fm.

Requests for information should be addressed to:

Zondervan, *Grand Rapids, Michigan 49530*

Library of Congress Cataloging-in-Publication Data

TerKeurst, Lysa.
    Unglued devotional : 60 days of imperfect progress / Lysa TerKeurst.
      p. cm.
    ISBN 978-0-310-32032-6 (softcover)
    1. Christian women—Prayers and devotions. I. Title.
BV4844.T43   2013
242'.643—dc23   2012034383

Published in association with the literary agency of Fedd & Company, Inc., Post Office Box 341973, Austin, TX 78734.

Cover design: Curt Diepenhorst
Cover photography: Helena Inkeri / Getty Images®
Interior design: Beth Shagene

Printed in the United States of America

13 14 15 16 17 18 /DCI/ 22 21 20 19 18 17 16 15 14 13 12 11 10 9 8 7 6 5

Contents

A Personal Word for You

Hi Friend,

I consider it a privilege for my words to be part of your devotional time during the coming weeks. As I write, I'm imagining where you'll be when reading this. In a quiet coffee shop sipping something warm and wonderful? Beside a pile of laundry in your toy-filled den? At an office desk during your lunch break?

Wherever you are, I give these words to you as my imperfect gift. God has taught me so much about making wise choices in the midst of raw emotions. I'm not as loud when I'm upset, and I'm less prone to stuff down bitterness when I get hurt. Here are the key words in this last sentence: "not as loud" and "less prone." I'm making progress, but, as you'll see in these pages, it's very much "imperfect progress."

And I'm okay with that. I'm okay with the fact that my life, my emotions, and my reactions are still messy at times. That's where grace steps in and wraps mercy around and around my heart, assuring me, "This, this hard stuff, is why you need a Savior. It's why you need to spend time with Him."

Time with Jesus. Yes, this is what I need and what I hope to help you find through these pages.

Each morning my mind is like a dry sponge. Whatever I soak up first is what I'll be most saturated with each day. And what I'm most saturated with each day is what I'll leak out on others when life's tough stuff squeezes me.

I want to leak patience, kindness, gentleness, and grace.

And I know you want this too. So, we choose to let our hearts and minds intersect with God's Word, and when we blow it, we can come back to our Bible and this devotional for help. Reassurance. Instruction. And more lavish grace.

I can't promise you that I'll be the hero of this book. No, not at all. But I can promise you'll find a friend who's been there, understands, and has learned some helpful wisdom.

So, grab a cup of coffee or another favorite beverage. I'll be right here with my iced green tea. As we venture through these pages and apply what we learn, we are going to gain more peace, honesty, and connection in our closest relationships. You are not trapped by the emotional cycles of your past. Hope for change is rising! These beautiful changes you've longed for are about to happen. So, turn afresh the pages of your life and this book and let's make some imperfect progress together.

Lysa TerKeurst

Time for a New Script

"For I am the LORD your God
who takes hold of your right hand and says to you,
Do not fear; I will help you."
(ISAIAH 41:13)

Thought for the Day: While feeling unglued is all I've really known, today my life can be different.

I'm sad because of the way I acted today. I'm disappointed in my lack of self-control. And the more I relive my emotionally driven tirade, the more my brain refuses sleep.

I have to figure this out. What is my problem? Why can't I seem to control my reactions? I stuff. I explode. And I don't know how to get a handle on this. But God help me if I don't get a handle on this. I will destroy the relationships I value most and weave into my life permanent threads of short-temperedness, shame, fear, and frustration. Is that what I really want? Do I want my headstone to read, "Well, on the days she was nice, she was really nice. But on the days she wasn't, rest assured, hell hath no fury like the woman who lies beneath the ground right here"?

No. That's not what I want. Not at all. I don't want the script of my life to be written that way.

So, at 2:08 a.m., I vow to do better tomorrow. But better proves elusive and my vow wears thin in the face of daily annoyances and other unpleasant realities. Tears slip, and I'm worn out from trying. Always trying.

I feel broken. Unglued, actually. I have vowed to do better at 2:08 a.m. and 8:14 a.m. and 3:37 p.m. and 9:49 p.m. and many other minutes in between. So why aren't things getting better? Why aren't my reactions tamer?

I know what it's like to praise God one minute and in the next minute yell and scream at my child—and then to feel both the burden of my destructive behavior and the shame of my powerlessness to stop it.

The emotional demands keep on coming. Unrelenting insecurity. Wondering if anyone appreciates me. Feeling tired, stressed, and hormonal.

Feeling unglued is really all I've ever known. And I'm starting to wonder if maybe it's all I'll ever be.

Those were the defeating thoughts I couldn't escape. Maybe you can relate. If you relate to my hurt, I pray you will also relate to my hope. While unglued is all I've really known, I believe that with God's help, today my life can be different. That's my personal revelation of hope. The pages of this devotional are my hope journal. A place of tender mercies and grace given so many times it almost seems scandalous. How can our God be so patient? I don't know. But He is. Today, He's offering us the fresh start our souls desperately need. Our key verse from Isaiah 41 promises He will help us.

We can be different. A slate wiped clean. A page crisp white. A chance to start rewriting the old scripts of past failures. For me. For you. Together.

We can do this.

God, thank You that this is a new twenty-four hours. Today, I want to believe I can start writing a new script for my life. Help me to overcome the disbelief I have because of my past failures. Amen.

DAY 2

Imperfect Progress

Practice these things;
immerse yourself in them,
so that all may see your progress.
(1 TIMOTHY 4:15 ESV)

Thought for the Day:
Just because something is hard doesn't mean it's impossible.

What kept me from making changes with my raw emotions was the feeling I wouldn't do it perfectly. I knew I'd still mess up and come unglued. Sometimes we girls think if we don't make instant progress, then real change isn't coming. But that's not so. There is a beautiful reality called *imperfect progress*. The day I realized the glorious hope of this kind of imperfect change is the day I gave myself permission to believe I really could be different.

Imperfect changes are slow steps of progress wrapped in grace ... imperfect progress. And good heavens, I need lots of that. So I dared to write this in my journal:

Progress. Just make progress. It's okay to have setbacks and the need for do-overs. It's okay to draw a line in the sand and start over again — and again. Just make sure you're moving the line forward. Move forward. Take baby steps, but at least take steps that keep you from being stuck. Then change will come. And it will be good.

These honest words enabled me to begin rewriting my story. Not that I erased what came before, but I stopped rehashing it and turned the page afresh. Eventually, I started blogging about my raw emotions and imperfect changes. In response, I got comments whispering, "Me too."

"Being unglued, for me, comes from a combination of anger and fear," wrote Kathy. "I think part of it is learned behavior. This is how my father was." Courtney honestly admitted, "I come unglued when I feel out of control because my kids are screaming or fighting or whining or negotiating and won't listen. I like silence, calm, obedience, and control. When it's not going 'my way,' I come unglued and freak out and it goes quiet. And then the regret comes."

And the comments kept coming, all of them expressing the exact same struggle, the same frustration, and the same need for hope. Women with kids and women without kids. Women caring for aging parents and women struggling with being the aging parent. Women working in the home and outside the home. So many women whose daily circumstances differed but whose core issues were the same.

I realized then that maybe other women could make some imperfect progress too. And a book idea was born from that simple realization. But I had to laugh at the irony of it. I had just published a book called *Made to Crave* that dealt with what goes into my mouth. Now I was writing a book called *Unglued* to deal with what comes out of my mouth. Obviously my mouth gets me into lots of trouble!

This *Unglued* journey is about my imperfect progress. It's an honest admission that this struggle of reining in how I react has been hard for me. But hard doesn't mean impossible.

How hard something is often depends on your vantage point. For example, consider the shell of an egg. Looking at it from the outside, we know an eggshell is easily broken. But if you're looking at that same shell from the inside, it seems an impenetrable fortress. It's impossible for the raw white and tender yolk to penetrate the hardness of the eggshell. But given time and the proper incubation, the white and yolk develop into a new life that breaks through the shell and shakes itself free. And in the end, we can see that the hard work of cracking the shell was good for the new baby chick. The shell actually provided a place for new life to grow, and then enabled the chick to break forth in strength.

Might the same be true for our hard places? Might all this struggle with our raw emotions and unglued feelings have the exact same potential for new life and new strength?

I think so. I know so. I've seen so.

Mother Teresa is quoted as saying, "Be faithful in small things because it is in them that your strength lies." Make some small imperfect progress today and discover your potential for new life and new strength.

God, this process is revealing to me my greater need for You each day. Please help me to take steps toward making imperfect progress today. Amen.

DAY 3

God, I'm a Little Mad
and a Lot Confused

Trust in the LORD with all your heart
and lean not on your own understanding;
in all your ways submit to him,
and he will make your paths straight.

(PROVERBS 3:5–6)

Thought for the Day:
God is big enough to handle our honest feelings.

Kick off your shoes and get ready to get gut-honest. When God doesn't seem to be answering our prayers, it can be hard. Sometimes, downright awful.

One minute, I'm determined to trust God. The next, I feel myself questioning God. The "why" questions tumble in so hard. My heart hurts. My tears fall. And in those raw moments I just feel a little mad and a lot confused.

Ever been there?

I don't want to oversimplify what to do in these times. Facing issues that never seem to stop is tough. Really tough. Especially those situations where the answers aren't easy or clean-cut. But I have discovered three things that help me when God seems silent.

1. Press into God when you want to pull away.

When I really want to hear from God, but He seems silent, I sometimes find I want to disengage from my normal spiritual activities. Skip church. Put my Bible on the shelf. And let more and more time lapse between prayers.

But pulling away only makes things worse. God says, "You will seek me and find me when you seek me with all your heart" (Jeremiah 29:13). All my heart includes the parts that are broken. Bring it all to God.

He can handle your honesty and will respond. But we have to go where truth is. Go to church. Listen to praise music. Read the Bible. Memorize verses. And keep talking to God.

2. Praise God out loud when you want to get lost in complaints.

In the midst of whatever you're facing, find simple things for which to praise God. I don't mean thank Him for the hard stuff. I mean thank Him for the other simple, good things you still experience. A child's laugh. A bush that blooms. The warmth of a blanket. The gift of this breath and then the next.

Scripture reminds me that praise leads to newness: "He put a new song in my mouth, a song of praise to our God; many will see and fear and will trust in the LORD" (Psalm 40:3 NASB). We can literally find new words with which to process life in a more positive way when we choose to praise God instead of complain.

3. Put yourself in the company of truth.

That friend who speaks truth? Listen to her. Stay connected to her. Let her speak truth into your life even when you're tired of hearing it. As Proverbs 12:26 (NASB) encourages, "The righteous is a guide to his neighbor." Stand in the shadow of her faith when you feel your own faith is weak. Let her lead you back to God time and time again.

It's okay to feel a little mad and a lot confused. Our God is big enough to handle our honest feelings. But don't let your feelings lead you away from God or away from His truth. Press into Him. Praise Him. And put yourself in the company of truth. As you stay with God in these ways, you will be ready to receive His answer when it comes.

Dear Lord, thank You for understanding me, even when I'm mad or confused. I pray I would daily be intentional in coming close to You and praising You. Help me to find a good friend whom I can trust to speak truth into my life. In Jesus' name. Amen.

Feeling Guilty?

For you created my inmost being;
you knit me together in my mother's womb.
I praise you because I am fearfully and wonderfully made;
your works are wonderful, I know that full well.
(PSALM 139:13 – 14)

Thought for the Day:
Sometimes I feel guiltier for what I'm not than thankful for what I am.

I gathered the restaurant bags, sighed, and crammed them into the overstuffed trash can. A friend had sent me a recipe that day that involved peeling and chopping and simmering. I imagined her trash can full of fresh veggie peelings and other things that proved her kitchen produced way more homemade goodness than mine.

And a little thread of guilt wrapped around my heart.

Sometimes I feel guiltier for what I'm not than thankful for what I am.

But there was sweet grace waiting for me in a little yogurt shop that night. My daughter had asked if I would come and speak to a Bible study she was helping organize. "Mom, I think a lot of people are going to show up."

So instead of cooking that night, I ordered out. Again. And I drove to the yogurt shop with a girl whose heart was full of excitement and expectation.

People were everywhere. Young people. Invited people. And parents. Nearly two hundred people packed inside the yogurt shop and overflowed outside. My daughter smiled.

I took the microphone and spoke from my heart. I told my story. I taught truth. I invited the people to let Jesus be the Lord of their hearts.

And many who had never done so said yes to God that night. A teen girl who tried to commit suicide last year. She stood to accept Jesus. A young man with tears in his eyes. He stood to accept Jesus. A mom and a dad. They stood to accept Jesus. Along with many others.

In the yogurt shop.

With a woman whose trash can was filled with take-out bags and who isn't the greatest cook, but a woman who wants to learn to be more thankful for what I am than guilty for what I'm not.

Maybe you are the friend with the veggie peelings in the trash can and steaming homemade goodness on the table.

Celebrate that.

Or maybe you are like me. And your gifts are less tasty.

Celebrate that.

And cut the threads of guilt with the edge of grace.

Dear Lord, You made me in Your image—and that is something I seem to forget daily. Please help me remember to celebrate and live in who You made me to be, and not dwell on what I wish I were. In Jesus' name. Amen.

DAY 5

Self-Control

*Like a city whose walls are broken through
is a person who lacks self-control.*
(PROVERBS 25:28)

Thought for the Day: The answer to keeping God's power with me and working in me to produce self-control is letting His Word get inside me.

Have you ever been in a discussion with a loved one when something snarky gets said and suddenly your blood pressure skyrockets, your nerves fray, and the worst version of you begs to come out?

Not that this ehhhhhver happens to me, of course.

Ahem.

Of course it happens to me. I live with other humans.

Whenever any kind of relationship conflict arises, my choice is whether to give the other person power to control my emotions.

When I react by yelling or flying off the handle or making a snappy comeback, I basically transfer my power to the other person. When I am void of power, I am void of self-control. So, it seems to me, if I'm going to remain self-controlled, I have to keep my power.

Now, when I say "my power," I don't mean something I conjure up myself. I am referring to God's power working in me. When I react according to God's Word, I feel that power. When I react contrary to God's Word, I feel powerless.

The prophet Isaiah provides a good reminder of what God Himself has said about tapping into His power, no matter what situation we are facing:

> "As the rain and the snow come down from heaven, and do not return to it without watering the earth and making it bud and flourish, so that it yields seed for the sower and bread for the eater, so is my word that goes out from my mouth: It will not return to me empty, but will accomplish what I desire and achieve the purpose for which I sent it."

> (Isaiah 55:10 – 11)

Did you catch that? The answer to keeping God's power with me and working in me to produce self-control is letting His Word get inside me. His Word seeping into my mind and my heart will accomplish things — good things, powerful things, things that help me display self-control.

So, all that to say, here's my new tactic: When I'm facing a situation where someone is getting on my last good nerve, I'm going to start quoting God's Word in the present tense. For example, if one of my sweet children starts acting *not so sweet*, I might say aloud (or silently, depending on the situation) words based on 1 Peter 5:6 – 8:

In this moment I'm choosing to be self-controlled and alert. Your actions are begging me to yell and lose control. I do have an enemy, but that enemy is not you. The devil is prowling and roaring and look-ing to devour me through my own lack of control right now. But I am God's girl. That's right, I am. I am going to humbly and quietly let God have His way in me right now. And when I do this, God will lift me and my frayed nerves up from this situation and fill me with a much better reaction than what I can give you right now. So give me just a few minutes and then we'll calmly talk about this.

Girl, that's some power right there.

And it will make you shine with so much self-control that your kids, your friends, your spouse, your coworkers won't know what to do with you.

Can you imagine what might happen if we wrote out power-ful responses from God's Word on three-by-five cards and pulled them out every time we found ourselves in a situation? Take the first step by starting with one of the verses we've looked at today. Tuck that card away in your purse or put it someplace you will see it frequently.

I love being God's girl. Don't you?

Dear Lord, thank You that Your Word applies to so many areas of my life. Sometimes I really struggle with self-control and I need Your power to help me react in a graceful, godly way. In Jesus' name. Amen.

DAY 6

The Root of My Rot

Do not conform any longer to the pattern of this world,
but be transformed by the renewing of your mind.
Then you will be able to test and approve what God's will is—
his good, pleasing and perfect will.
(ROMANS 12:2)

Thought for the Day:
How we react is a crucial gauge of what's really going on inside us.

Last week, I got all twisted up and bent out of shape. And, honey, everyone in my house knew Mama wasn't happy. I tried everything to usher gentleness back into my tone and my temper.

I quoted verses.

I rebuked Satan.

I bossed my feelings around with truth.

I even tried to take a nap.

But none of these activities soothed me.

One of my people had done something to introduce a smell into my home that not even three Yankee candles could mask. And I am supersensitive to smells. Like hyper-crazy sensitive.

As the mysterious, awful smell continued to waft through my home, assaulting my nasal passages, I couldn't for the life of me figure out what it was or where it was coming from.

I lit candles, I sprayed stuff, I even covered my nose with the edge of my shirt ... but I still smelled it.

Finally, I realized my daughter had placed a bathroom trash can onto the middle of my bedroom floor and propped open the flip-up lid so she could throw away scraps of paper as she worked on a school project. Something had obviously been thrown away in that forgotten trash can that had surpassed gross and moved into the final stages of rot.

Or something had crawled up into that can and died.

I didn't have the heart to find out what it was; I just knew the can had to go. Immediately.

The smell was an outside indication of an internal situation. And the trash can wasn't the only thing that stunk that night. So did my attitude. My reaction was an outside indication of an internal situation.

The reason I couldn't be soothed by quoting Scripture verses, bossing my feelings, rebuking Satan, or even taking a nap is because God wanted me to be aware of my stink ... something inside of me that was gross ... a place starting to rot. I had some bitterness I'd stuffed and tried to pretend wasn't there. I'd been hurt by a friend and didn't want to confront the issue or forgive the person who had hurt me. But the rot was there and the stink from deep within my heart kept spilling out.

God didn't want me to temporarily mask the situation by feeling better in the moment. He wanted me to address the root of my rot—to see it, admit it, expose it, let Him clean it up, and shut it down. Immediately.

A little rot can spread fast and furiously if not dealt with swiftly and seriously.

That's why it's so crucial to pay attention to our reactions today. How we react is a crucial gauge of what's really going on inside us. When people or issues or situations bump into our happy, it's not wrong to feel annoyed. But if that annoyance leads to a reaction out of proportion to the issue at hand, we can bank on the fact that this eruption has a root of rot.

Here are some telltale signs of roots of rot:

- I throw out statements like, *You always ... You never ... Why can't we ever ...*
- I start gathering ammunition from past situations to build my case.
- I use words and a tone outside my normal character.
- I justify my reaction by pointing out how hard my life is right now.
- I demand an apology, all the while knowing I should be giving one.

These are not fun to admit, but here's the beauty of the situation: The quicker we see a root of rot, the quicker we can get rid of the stink and move forward.

Dear Lord, thank You for bringing to light the rotting areas of my life. Help me to address these areas with Your grace and truth. In Jesus' name. Amen.

DAY 7

Rainy Days and Mondays

"Forget the former things; do not dwell on the past.
See, I am doing a new thing! Now it springs up;
do you not perceive it? I am making a way
in the wilderness and streams in the wasteland."

(ISAIAH 43:18 – 19)

Thought for the Day: The best thing for me to do is to position my heart in a place where I can experience God.

This devotion is for one of "those days." Yes, that kind.

If you're having a tough start to your day, I understand. Me too. I've been up since 3:00 a.m. and will seriously need some Holy Spirit empowering to make it until bedtime.

I'm tired. But I'm also feeling under attack. I know you know what I mean.

Satan typically throws everything he can at us to try to make us start off our days on an unglued footing. There will be kids who don't feel well. Marital tiffs. Unexpected demands that pop up on our to-do lists. Dogs that run away. And a mountain of laundry to be done.

And I just might have a little personal experience this morning with each and every item on that list. Lovely.

On days like this, I have to stand on what I know to be true instead of being whisked away in a sea of emotion. Here are three things I'm preaching to myself this morning:

1. I'm not a slave to my feelings. I'm the boss of them.

2. Just because I've had a few bad moments this morning doesn't make me a bad person.

3. This too shall pass. In the meantime, the best thing for me is to position my heart in a place where I can experience God.

And trust me, there is no better place to experience God than by opening His Word and then opening my heart to that Word. Which is exactly what I'm tempted to put off doing on an off-track day. But then I read a verse like our key verse: "Forget the former things; do not dwell on the past. See, I am doing a new thing! Now it springs up; do you not perceive it? I am making a way in the wilderness and streams in the wasteland" (Isaiah 43:18–19). See? God will make a way on this off-track day to put me and my unglued heart back on track.

I'm deciding to boss my feelings, realize bad moments don't define me, and look for the way God is already turning this day around.

Dear Lord, I want to remember that You are always here for me—on good days and bad. Help me to enjoy the good ones and receive Your help on the not-so-good ones. In Jesus' name. Amen.

DAY 8

Reactor or Responder?

For God did not give us a spirit of timidity,
but a spirit of power,
of love and of self-discipline.
(2 TIMOTHY 1:7)

Thought for the Day: In the situations where I want to become unglued, I always have the choice to be a reactor or a responder.

I recently heard a story about a famous woman in the midst of an unglued reaction. She was in a restaurant having dinner with friends when a server spilled some spaghetti on her dress. She was distraught. Beyond distraught, actually. She shoved the server and became so belligerent, she was asked to leave. Later, the server sued this woman and won hundreds of thousands of dollars.

Crazy, right?

And here's the thing—her unglued reaction didn't un-spill the spaghetti from her dress! In the end, she had a stained dress, a ruined reputation, and was out hundreds of thousands of dollars.

31

While it's easy for me to shake my head, I dare not. I'll be honest, I can be the queen of wanting to react. I haven't ever shoved anyone, but I sure have whispered under my breath. Let me loose on something unfair, unjust, or just plain rude, and I can sure find some fight in me. Add to that a rush of adrenaline, and somebody had better be hoping I've read my Bible that day!

Only God can rein in my natural reactions. He is my primary source of power, love, and self-discipline. So I've devised a series of questions that helps me tap into that source when I feel a reaction coming on. There's a big difference between being a reactor and a responder — and I want to be a responder.

Q: *Do I want to escalate this conflict or dissipate it?*
A reactor escalates the conflict.
A responder dissipates the conflict.

Q: *Do I want more trouble or more grace in my life?*
A reactor adds trouble on top of trouble.
A responder adds grace on top of grace.

Q: *Do I want to be known as harsh or gentle?*
A reactor either spews emotion or masters the silent treatment.
A responder gives a gentle answer.

Q: *Do I want to get my own way or help find a resolution?*
A reactor only sees things her way.
A responder realizes there are always two sides to every issue.

Q: *Which do I care more about — demanding my rights or displaying right choices?*
A reactor demands her right to be right.
A responder is more concerned about making right choices before God.

If you struggle with being a reactor, I understand. I'm not saying becoming a responder is easy or that it can happen overnight. But it is possible, and we can make progress.

Father, today I want to be a woman who responds to people with love and grace because it allows me to be a better representative of You. Please guide me through every obstacle, steering me to react in a way that honors Your name. Amen.

DAY 9

Pretending I'm Fine,
Proving I'm Right

But the wisdom that comes from heaven is first of all pure;
then peace-loving, considerate, submissive,
full of mercy and good fruit, impartial and sincere.
(JAMES 3:17)

Thought for the Day: If I catch myself pretending or proving, I know
I'm processing my hurt the wrong way.

If someone says something or does something that hurts me, what
is the godly response? Is it to pretend that everything is fine so I
can keep the peace? Or is it to confront the person to prove how
wrong she is?

Neither.

If ever I catch myself pretending or proving, I know I'm processing my hurt the wrong way.

The right way is approaching this situation with soul integrity

—responding in a way that's not only honest but peacemaking. James 3:17 says, "But the wisdom that comes from heaven is first of all pure [honest]; then peace-loving ..." Yes, I want this kind of wisdom, this soul integrity. I want to be honest and peacemaking at the same time. But how?

Real honesty. Not all honest expressions of my feelings are real honesty. You see, my honest feelings may not be truthful assessments of the situation. I can be honest with how I feel and still exaggerate or misinterpret what is true. I can feel justified in being blatant about my feelings—not hiding a thing—and prideful for being so real, all under the guise of being honest enough not to stuff.

But in reality, honesty that isn't true isn't honesty at all. It may just be emotional spewing. That's why we need peacemaking honesty—honesty reined in by the Holy Spirit—if we're going to have authentic soul integrity.

So if I want real honesty, I have to ask the Holy Spirit to show me real truth. I need to see things from the other person's perspective. I need to ask questions of that person with the desire to better understand instead of throwing out statements of accusation. Ultimately, my goal should be to add peacemaking to my honesty.

Real peacemaking. At the same time, it must also grieve God to see plastic versions of peacemaking that aren't reined in by honesty. That's what we do when we stuff and pretend everything is okay. The upside of stuffing is that we have the semblance of peacemakers. But when we do so at the expense of honesty, we harbor a corrosive bitterness that will eventually emerge. Either it will erode our health and later present itself in a host of emotional and physical anxiety-induced illnesses, or it will accumulate over time and surprise everyone when the peacemaker eventually erupts. Saying "I'm fine" to keep the peace, when we're really not fine, isn't honest.

Sometimes dishonesty comes in the form of saying things that aren't true. But it's also dishonest when we fail to say things that are true.

It may seem godly in the moment, but it's false godliness. Truth and godliness always walk hand in hand. The minute we divorce one from the other, we stray from soul integrity and give a foothold to the instability that inevitably leads to coming unglued.

Yes, we're after soul integrity — honesty that is also peacemaking that leads to godliness. This soul integrity brings balance to unglued reactions. It makes us true peacemakers — people who aren't proving or pretending but rather honestly demonstrating what they are experiencing in a godly manner. And being a true peacemaker reaps a harvest of great qualities in our lives: right things, godly things, healthy things.

Dear Lord, through You I am able to bring all my exploding and stuffing under Your authority and truth. Thank You for Your Holy Spirit who gives me the wisdom to move beyond my reactions. Help me lean on You. In Jesus' name. Amen.

DAY 10

The Exploder Who
Shames Herself

Finally, brothers and sisters, whatever is true,
whatever is noble, whatever is right, whatever is pure,
whatever is lovely, whatever is admirable — if anything
is excellent or praiseworthy — think about such things.
(PHILIPPIANS 4:8)

Thought for the Day: Sip the shame so you won't have to guzzle gallons of unwanted regret.

The first line of the email was "Shame on you."

Lovely.

It was from a fellow middle school parent who was deeply offended that her daughter hadn't been invited to my daughter's birthday party. Take note of two words in that last sentence that strike fear deep within the hearts of many, many mothers: *middle school.* Need I say more? Glory be.

Never mind that Hope had been having problems with this girl hurting her feelings all year. Never mind we'd decided to invite only the girls in her homeroom class, of which this girl was not part. And never mind we wished we could invite this girl, but the fear of her repeating the hurt she'd caused in school sent Hope into a crying fit.

So we didn't invite her. I'm not saying this was the right decision. But honestly, it wasn't done out of spite at all. We'd done so many things to reach out and extend love to this girl, and Hope was just completely worn out from continually getting nothing but hurt back. It was a tough decision and one I didn't make lightly.

But, still, I got this email. Not only did I get the shame-on-you email, but this other mom was clear about her plans to have Hope called into the principal's office and reminded to be kind to her daughter.

I don't know what the official definition of a *twit* is. Nor am I completely sure *twit* is a real word. However, when you feel all twisted up, with irritation sprinkled on top, *twit* seems fitting.

So there I was in a twit right at the start of a new day.

Typically, I am a middle school parent who stays out of the drama. And I readily admit when my kids need to be corrected and redirected. But on this day I could envision myself zinging the person who hurt me with the perfect comeback. I mentally weighed all the many reasons I was perfectly justified in leveling the scales of hurt.

She dumped a bucket of hurt on me. The scale tipped heavy on my side. Therefore, I should dump a bucket of hurt on her. Then the scales would be even and my twit would dissipate in this balance of hurt equality. But something in my spirit didn't feel any better after I mentally walked through this leveling of the scales.

I felt heavy.

In this instance, I was about to be an exploder who would later feel shame for not acting more like someone who really loves Jesus and follows Him. Being able to identify my tendency helped me see in advance the downside of the reaction I was about to have. I imagined myself feeling the shame of exploding on this woman and I didn't like how it felt. I didn't want shame to be my reality.

I'll sometimes say to myself, "Sip the shame so you won't have to guzzle the regret." In other words, taste a little bit of the shame of what will be if you let it all rip before you find yourself drowning in gallons of unwanted regret.

Sipping the shame of what would be if I let my raw emotions have their way helped me not to explode. And that's good. But I still had some processing to do to get the hurtful feelings to dissipate. The last thing we want to do is trade our unhealthy exploding for unhealthy stuffing. Remember, the balance between the two is soul integrity where our honesty is godly.

Dear Lord, thank You for Your patience as I try to make progress with my reactions. Please help me to be truly honest but full of grace with those You have put in my life. In Jesus' name. Amen.

DAY 11

The Exploder Who Blames Others

Therefore be clear minded and self-controlled
so that you can pray.
(1 PETER 4:7)

Thought for the Day:
Feelings are indicators, not dictators.

Every now and then I attempt to be "that mom." You know, the one who wields a glue gun whilst craftifying something worthy of a showcase display at the Hobby Lobby. And the one who joyfully reads aloud to her children without being sneaky and skipping pages. Yes, her.

But it never works out for me.

Take, for example, the brilliant time I decided to attend a book warehouse clearance sale. I loaded up my kids and decided this was the perfect time to help my people fall in love with books. I wrongly figured a sale could help anyone feel the literary love. Not so.

My kids couldn't have cared less about the books.

What they wanted was in a crate off to the side of all the bookshelves. The brightly colored packages were laced with promises. I plucked from my kids' hands one that claimed to contain the coolest-ever science experiment. Anytime a brightly colored package uses the words *cool* and *experiment* on the front, a mother should beware. Especially when said package is marked down to one dollar. She should be very wise and tell her children, "No."

But, tired from all efforts to convince them to love books, I rationalized that since we'd dedicated our morning to this sale, we should at least walk out with something educational. So I bought several of the kits.

Sea monkeys. That's what the kits were supposed to grow. Key words: *supposed to*. My kids were beyond excited to get this party started. Into the container went the chemicals, the water, the little food crystals, and plastic green trees upon which the sea monkeys could play once they hatched.

It's at this point I should let you know that this is one of those good news/bad news stories. Yes, ma'am, which would you like first?

The good news ... something did hatch.

The bad news ... it wasn't sea monkeys.

After leaving the experiment overnight, I woke to find my kitchen invaded by the biggest, nastiest, hairiest giant flies you have ever seen. I'm not sure if our sea monkeys had a mutation situation going on or if some sort of larvae had gotten into the packages and eaten our sea monkeys.

Either way, it was awful.

The moral of this story is simple. Some moms are equipped by the hand of God to be "that mom." They have been formed with the three-C gene — Cooking, Crafting, and Cleaning come easily and naturally to them.

Others of us have been delightfully chosen to provide the comic relief necessary to keep this world entertained. And to keep future therapists in business.

I know this story sounds funny now, but at the time it was yet one more thing that excluded me from belonging to the good mom club. My internal good mom/bad mom dialogue tormented me:

Good moms grow sea monkeys. Bad moms grow nasty flies.

Wait! Good moms don't even buy sea monkey kits at a book sale. Bad moms struggle with telling their kids no and give in too easily.

Good moms get on the Internet and figure out how to turn a fly debacle into an enriching science lesson for their kids. Bad moms kill the stupid flies and hide all evidence of that from their kids.

And on and on the dialogue went. And with each assurance I was a bad mom, my emotions ratcheted higher and higher. On a stress scale from 1 to 10, I could have been hovering around 4, but then this conversation in my head pushed me all the way up to 7. Add to that a kid squabble over who licked whose toast at breakfast and the fact I couldn't find my cell phone, and I was all the way up to 9.8, ready to explode and blame anyone and everyone who had the misfortune to be nearby. What I felt was anger. What I needed was self-control.

I'm trying to better understand this whole concept of self-control. The Bible includes many verses about the subject, among them Proverbs 25:28, Galatians 5:23, and 1 Peter 4:7. But it's hard to display self-control when someone else does things out of my control that yank my emotions into a bad place. So here's a little tidbit I'm learning. When someone else's actions or statements threaten to pull me into a bad place, I have a choice. I do. It may not feel like

I have a choice. In fact, it may feel like I am a slave to my feelings —but I'm not. Remember, feelings are indicators, not dictators. Feelings can indicate there is a situation I need to deal with, but they shouldn't dictate how I react. I have a choice.

Dear Lord, when conversations, situations, and distractions in my day threaten to take over my emotions, please help me remember my feelings are indicators, not dictators. I want to quiet my inner dialogue and replace my anxiety with Your comfort and truth. In Jesus' name. Amen.

DAY 12

The Stuffer Who Builds Barriers

And God is able to make all grace abound to you,
so that having all sufficiency in all things at all times,
you may abound in every good work.
(2 CORINTHIANS 9:8 ESV)

Thought for the Day: It's unfair of me to use my expectations as the standard for someone else's behavior or hold it against her when she doesn't live up to my hopes.

What often opens the door of conflict in my relationships is expectations. There are two kinds of expectations: realistic and unrealistic. Unrealistic expectations are things another person isn't able or willing to do for me. I have to let go of these. Certainly God can either change that person or change me by rearranging my desires. In the meantime, it's unfair of me to use my expectations as the standard for other people's behavior or hold it against them when they don't live up to my hopes.

Realistic expectations, on the other hand, are things I *can* reasonably expect another person to do for me. Of course, it's important to discern how to communicate these expectations with gentleness and at the right time. Timing is key.

My pastor's wife, Holly Furtick, recently told me how she discerns the timing of such conversations with her husband, Steven. She prays specifically that God will make it clear to her when the time is right to have non-emotionally charged conversations of gentle confrontation or clarification. As she's running errands, fixing dinner, or flipping through her fashion magazines (the girl loves fashion!), she prays for God to make the timing clear. And He does!

She'd been wanting to talk to Steven about something that had been bothering her, but she didn't want it to become a big deal. She determined it was a realistic expectation on her part, so she committed to pray for the right timing. A few weeks later, she and Steven were coming home from a trip. They'd had a great time. Suddenly, he slid a piece of paper her way and said, "Write down three things I could do better as your husband."

Holly smiled. This was exactly what she'd been praying for —but even better! Her husband was the one who paved the way for a healthy conversation. God doesn't always work so quickly in answering our timing prayers, but what a comfort and encouragement to see how God paved the way for a "clarifying expectations" conversation.

Why not take your expectations and your need for discernment about them to God in prayer? Why not ask Him to get involved? Holly's example inspired me and has given me yet another tool to keep me from stuffing and building barriers. Again, I won't minimize how hard these things can be. But imperfect progress is possible and gets us unstuck from unrealistic expectations that can so easily lead to barrier building in our relationships.

Dear Lord, thank You for going before me in every difficult situation. I want to pause and wait on Your leading before I speak. But I do want to speak instead of stuffing and building barriers. Teach me to seek You and know the right way to communicate in my situation. In Jesus' name. Amen.

DAY 13

The Stuffer Who Collects Retaliation Rocks

A hot-tempered person stirs up conflict,
but the one who is patient calms a quarrel.
(PROVERBS 15:18)

Thought for the Day:
Am I trying to prove I'm right or improve this relationship?

When I can feel an argument brewing, I have to remember that my goal is to tackle the issue, not the person.

When I tackle an issue, I ask questions. These questions help me shift from trying to prove I am right to trying to improve the relationship. When I set out to prove I'm right, it leads to conflict escalation. When I determine to improve the relationship, it leads to conflict resolution.

Here are some questions that have helped me to redirect my focus from proving myself to improving the relationship:

- Can you help me understand why you feel this way?
- Can we both agree to stick to the issue at hand and not pull in past issues?
- What is a desired outcome in this situation?
- How can we meet in the middle on this issue?
- What is something good that can come out of this issue — something that will improve our relationship moving forward?

Of course, these have to be asked with the right tone and an honest desire to better understand the other person. (Trust me, I've asked with a snarky attitude and seriously impeded any positive progress!) But said in the right tone, it's so much better to throw out a gentle question than a bitter, condemning rock.

My husband, Art, and I have renamed our fights. We now call them "growth opportunities." But I don't want to give the wrong impression and end all cheerio. While Art and I are doing great right now and have had fewer growth opportunities lately, they always seem to be right around the corner. So please hear my heart: I'm not saying any of this is easy. But isn't it good to think about and work on healthy processing strategies? After all, we are the ones who benefit from them. Our relationships will improve. Our outlooks will be more positive. We'll start to see biblical truths coming alive in our lives, which will strengthen our relationship with God. And we'll learn to attack the issues rather than attacking each other.

Dear Lord, You are all grace. And I need all grace — to give it and receive it, especially when dealing with "growth opportunities." Instead of lobbing condemnation, I choose today to offer up gentleness. In Jesus' name. Amen.

DAY 14

Ruined for Good

Fools show their annoyance at once,
but the prudent overlook an insult.
(PROVERBS 12:16)

Thought for the Day: I have to make the choice every day to interrupt my fleshly tendencies of yelling and getting angry over minor things.

If you have kids, then I'm sure you've felt the frustration of having things ruined. Maybe you've experienced grape juice on the carpet, scratches on hardwood floors, permanent ink on your favorite shirt, or something similar.

My daughter, Ashley, once went up the stairway with a crayon putting tick marks on our freshly painted walls with each step she took. Then she dragged the crayon all the way down the hall to her room. Yes, I said freshly painted walls. I wanted to pull my hair out by the roots!

I'd like to be a mom who handles mishaps and messes with a

49

graceful, "That's okay, dear." But I'm wired with firecrackers in my blood. So I have to make the choice to let the Holy Spirit rein me in. This means getting into God's Word every day and praying for Him to help me display grace, patience, and self-control when I want to do the exact opposite.

I have to make the choice every day to invite God's Spirit to interrupt my fleshly tendencies of yelling and getting so angry over minor things. As Proverbs 12:16 says, I don't want to be a fool that shows my annoyance at once. I want to be a prudent, wise woman. I want to be a woman who doesn't constantly regret my reactions later.

God helps me with this through perspective changers. He shows me a different way to look at and process things that trigger my emotions. In response to my frustration with my kids ruining things, He gave me a sweet change of perspective that improved my outlook and diffused my anger.

While visiting my husband's parents, I took a liking to a writing desk in their home. I mentioned to Art's mom that I'd love to have it if she ever decided to get rid of it. But she was quick to tell me that she would never get rid of it because it was priceless.

She unlatched the fold-down lid to reveal what made this desk so special to her. In a little boy's handwriting, the letters A-R-T were scratched onto the surface. His name was forever carved onto her desk.

She admitted to being angry with Art when this happened years and years ago, but now the scratches that seemed to have ruined her desk are priceless treasures to her. Her little boy's handwriting is saved for her to cherish and remember. The desk had been ruined ... for good.

And I pray that remembering this story, this perspective change, makes me ruined for good as well.

Dear Lord, thank You for perspective changes that help us to see past the here and now so that we can see Your truth which sets us free. We are freed from anger, firecracker emotions, short fuses, and explosive tempers ... free to reveal the You in us! In Jesus' name. Amen.

DAY 15

Is My Pain Talking?

We take captive every thought
to make it obedient to Christ.
(2 CORINTHIANS 10:5)

Thought for the Day:
Our Lord doesn't whisper shameful condemnations.

Have you ever been in a situation where something little felt really big? Maybe a look from someone that suddenly makes you feel they don't like you at all. Or when someone doesn't return your phone call and you feel like it's an indication that you're not important.

Usually these things aren't true. The look was just a look with no hidden meaning. The missed phone call was just a slip on that person's to-do list. But if we're not careful, those misguided feelings can create issues that distract us, discourage us, and trigger past pain to start taunting us.

It happened to me on a certain Friday. My sister, Angee, and I got up at 3:00 a.m. and were in line at a certain retail establishment thirty minutes later. I know. I agree. That's crazy. But like a hunter stalking prey, I was after something. In this case, the buy-one-get-one-free washer and dryer. Angee was after a half-priced computer. When the store doors opened at 5:00 a.m., we both scored. Happiness abounded. Then we left to get some breakfast. This is the part of the story where the happiness faded.

In the drive-thru, my credit card was "not approved."

Let me get this straight. It *was* approved at the store just five minutes ago when I made a major purchase. But now for a little two-dollar bundle of egg, cheese, Canadian bacon, and English muffin, suddenly I'm *not* approved?

Not approved.

Not approved.

Ouch.

My sister wasn't fazed a bit. She whipped out cash, paid for my breakfast, and headed to the next store on our list. But those words "not approved" hung like a black cloud over my head. It bothered the stink out of me. I knew it was just some technical glitch, but that's not what it felt like.

When that girl leaned out of the drive-thru window and in a hushed tone said, "I'm sorry, ma'am, but your card keeps coming up as not approved," it felt personal. Really personal.

Suddenly, my past pain and current embarrassment started running its mouth inside my head. *You're nothing but a loser. You are unwanted. You are unloved. You are so disorganized. You are poor. You are not acceptable. You are not approved.* And all that pent-up yuck came spewing out on my kids later that afternoon.

I wish I could tie up this story in a nice bow and give you a pretty ending, but I can't. It was anything but pretty. I felt awful. And I went to bed wondering if the Lord Himself might come down and say, "Lysa TerKeurst, I have had enough of your immature reactions. You are no longer approved to be a Bible study teacher. Look at you!"

But that's not the Lord's voice. Our Lord doesn't whisper shameful condemnations. Convictions, yes. Condemnations, no.

As I stared wide-eyed into the darkness that enveloped the room, I whispered, "Give me Your voice, Jesus. I need to hear You above all this mess. If I don't hear You, I'm afraid this darkness is going to swallow me alive." Nothing came. I couldn't hear a thing.

So I had a choice. I could lie there in the dark replaying the awful events of the day, or I could turn the light on and read God's Word — His truth — which is the best thing to do when lies are swarming and attacking like a bunch of bloodthirsty mosquitoes. Lies flee in the presence of truth. And while reading God's truth that night didn't change the fact that I needed to make things right with my kids the next day, it sure did give me the courage to do so.

Dear Lord, please drown out the other voices ... please hush them ... and speak. I want to hear You above all the noise. In Jesus' name. Amen.

DAY 16

Condemnation vs. Conviction

But thanks be to God that, though you used to be slaves to sin,
you have come to obey from your heart the pattern of teaching
that has now claimed your allegiance. You have been set free
from sin and have become slaves to righteousness.

(ROMANS 6:17 – 18)

Thought for the Day: Condemnation defeats us.
Conviction unlocks the greatest potential for change.

When an airline recently lost my friend Holly's luggage, I was elected to go to the lost luggage office and see what could be done. The woman behind the counter saw me coming and held her hand up with a quick and cutting, "Don't even come in here until you've looked through the pile to the left."

So much for flying the friendly skies. I dutifully looked through the pile of homeless luggage and there wasn't one suitcase that looked anything like Holly's. So I proceeded to walk toward the office again.

"You didn't look!" yelled the woman behind the counter. "I told you to look *through* that pile."

I swallowed. Hard.

"I did look and I can guarantee you the piece of luggage I'm looking for isn't there," I said.

She rolled her eyes, motioned for me to approach her desk, and continued to do everything in her power to act as if losing Holly's suitcase was somehow my fault. I dealt with it. And dealt with it. And then got tired of dealing with it.

"Look," I snapped, "I am the customer here. Your airline lost our luggage. I wish I didn't have to be in this little office right now. But I am because it is your job to help me. And that's exactly what I need you to do ... your job."

I didn't raise my voice. But I did raise my intensity. I let the situation dictate my reaction, and I walked away feeling frustrated but justified. Until an hour later. I had this nagging sense I'd blown it. I started thinking of several of my gentle friends who never would have talked sharply or gotten caught up in their frustration: *Amy wouldn't have acted that way. Samantha would have used this as a golden opportunity to love the unlovely. Ann would have given so much grace, a revival would have taken place right there in the lost luggage office and years later this lady would be sharing her testimony of how everything changed the day that kind woman came to her office.*

Ugh. Shame slithered up close and whispered, "Look at you and all your Bible studying ... what good is it all? What good are you?" The heaviness in my soul left me with this sinking feeling that I would never really be able to change. And a familiar thought ran through a well-worn pattern in my brain: *I'll probably always be a slave to the raw emotions that catch me off guard.*

What a lie.

If you're believing this same lie, hang on to this truth: Just the fact that you're reading this book is a sign of great progress. Refuse to wallow in the depressing angst condemnation brings. On the other hand, embrace any conviction you feel. Condemnation defeats us. Conviction unlocks the greatest potential for change.

Conviction is a call to action, like the warning light on the dashboard of a car. What call to action can you embrace today to make even more imperfect progress? As for me, I'm deciding in advance to have compassion on people like the woman at the luggage counter. Obviously, something hard in her life caused her to display the attitude she did. When I imagine her hurt, I soften my reaction. Indeed, conviction leads to the greatest potential for me to change.

Dear Lord, show me where I have believed the lies that condemnation speaks. You've set me free, and I long to live in that truth. In Jesus' name. Amen.

DAY 17

Resist the Funk

Let your conversation be
always full of grace, seasoned with salt,
so that you may know how to answer everyone.
(COLOSSIANS 4:6)

Thought for the Day:
The reason I can give grace
is because I so desperately need it.

I like this verse. I really do. As a matter of fact, I've challenged my Proverbs 31 Ministries team that this is our focus — our honor code, if you will. It outlines how I want to honor God, honor others, and honor the opportunities entrusted to me each day. I told my team that an easy way to remember this verse is with three Gs:

Graceful: full of grace

Godly: seasoned with God's truth

Ready to Go: fully prepared to answer everyone

When I simplify this verse into three Gs, I can remember it. It interrupts me. It redirects me. But most of all, it challenges me. And the part that challenges me most is the "full of grace" part. My conversations should be full of grace. In other words, the bulk of my words should convey grace toward the person with whom I'm conversing. I don't know if you've ever tried this, but it's hard. Especially if that other person has yuck draped all over his or her attitude.

You know what I'm saying?

I love my kids and I wish motherhood were a string of beautiful, blissful days, but reality is sometimes very different. I had one of those altered-reality days recently when I knew things were going to be challenging with one of my daughters. I could tell she was going to push when I wanted to pull. She was going to go when I wanted to pause. She was going to take when I wasn't in the mood to give.

I just knew there was going to be a situation.

So, thinking on this verse, I said to myself, *Full of grace, Lysa. Absolutely full. Not partial. Not halfway. But all the way grace.*

When that inevitable situation arose, I measured out lavish grace with each response. Not that I didn't correct her—I did. But I did so in calm tones. I looked for ways to lovingly reassure her. I held her hand. And I kept quiet when my nerves were begging me to do otherwise.

I did really well ... for a couple of hours.

And then I lost it. Completely.

I was so discouraged.

But as I think back now, there was grace in that part of the experience too. I demonstrated that the reason I can give grace is because I so desperately need it. I asked my daughter's forgiveness, and I decided to resist my own funk that was begging me to sit and wallow in my messy humanity.

I dusted myself off and whispered, "God, help me. Please, please help me." And I took one more step toward the grace I so desperately want to demonstrate.

I don't know who puts grace to the test in your life, but how might things be different if, just for today, you decided to resist the funk and give grace a try with that person one more time?

Remember, grace doesn't have to be perfect to be good.

Dear Lord, thank You for Your amazing grace. I hope I show it in every conversation I have today. But when I blow it, thanks for giving me an extra measure of grace. In Jesus' name. Amen.

DAY 18

I Quit

*Godly sorrow brings repentance that leads to salvation
and leaves no regret, but worldly sorrow brings death.*
(2 CORINTHIANS 7:10)

Thought for the Day: "Jesus didn't die so we'd be sorry. He died and
then was resurrected so we'd be changed." — STEVEN FURTICK

My heart is stirred this morning to say it's time to quit. Not ministry. Not a relationship. But to quit being critical of someone I love very much. The crazy thing is, I'm not a critical person. But I've found myself slipping into a pattern of giving this person what she gives me.

She criticizes. So I've started criticizing back. A lot. And I'm feeling very convicted this morning that I need to model a different attitude and approach to life.

My pastor recently said something very convicting: "Jesus didn't die so we'd be sorry. He died and then was resurrected so we'd be changed."

Changed.

There is a big difference between being sorry and being changed. To be sorry means to feel bad. It's a temporary little prick of the heart. But change only comes when we're repentant. Being repentant is a deeper conviction to actually correct and transform our behavior—our habit—our unglued reactions.

The apostle Paul writes, "Godly sorrow brings repentance that leads to salvation and leaves no regret, but worldly sorrow leads to death" (2 Corinthians 7:10). *Sorrow that leaves no regret*—those are powerful and challenging words.

I want to live a life of no regrets. And I think today is a really good day to address something that could lead to a big ol' pile of regret. So each time I'm feeling the need to criticize, I'm going to see it as a call to flip my words to encouragement. I might still need to address some issues with this person, but I will do it by pointing out her strengths and the responsibilities that come with those strengths rather than constantly focusing on weaknesses.

For example, "You are an influencer! Have you noticed that when you are happy others are happy, but when you are negative, it really affects those around you? I need your help to keep things positive today. Do you think you can accept this leadership role? How can you be a positive influence in this situation?"

I'm not naive enough to think this will be easy. I will need grace. This person will need grace.

But at least if I'm aware of how I need to change, I can set change in motion.

Are you up for quitting some old habit, negative attitude, or wrong tendency? What can you quit today?

Dear Lord, I'm ready to quit. Instead of critical words, I want to speak kind and encouraging ones. Please give me the help I need to make this shift. In Jesus' name. Amen.

DAY 19

When My Heart
Feels Desperate

When I said, "My foot is slipping,"
your love, O LORD, supported me.
When anxiety was great within me,
your consolation brought joy to my soul.

(PSALM 94:18–19)

Thought for the Day: The only thing that stops the desperation, the uncertainties, the insecurities, the twirling, is for the Spirit of God to cover my heart and make it still.

If you've ever heard me give my testimony, you know part of what I talk about is being a little girl twirling around next to my daddy wishing I could know for sure that he loved me. In his own way, I think he did love me. But something was broken in our relationship that left me feeling desperate for reassurance.

Over the years, God has healed my heart in miraculous ways.

He has whispered to me all those things I wished my earthly father would have said. I know for sure God's love for me is deep, unwavering, and certain. But there are times I still catch myself twirling. Crying out. Wishing I could feel totally secure. Hating my insecurities. And mad that this struggle I thought was over has surfaced again.

Maybe it always will. And maybe that's not such a bad thing. For it keeps me desperate for a reassurance I can't get any other way.

I can stand in an arena with thousands of people clapping for the message I just gave . . . and still feel my heart desperately twirling.

I can hear my husband tell me a hundred times that he loves me and no, my butt isn't big . . . and still feel my heart desperately twirling.

I can conquer my food demons and finally fit back into my skinny jeans . . . and still feel my heart desperately twirling.

The only thing that stops the desperation, the uncertainties, the insecurities, the twirling, is for the Spirit of God to cover my heart and make it still. As Psalm 94 says, "When anxiety was great within me, your consolation brought joy to my soul." The blanket of His presence is my consolation and His protection is the only perfect fit for the deep creases and crevices carved inside me.

I don't know what tough things you've been through in your life, sweet sister, but I do know brokenness is universal. We all have life issues that can trigger unglued reactions, deep insecurities, and our own personal twirling about looking for reassurance.

But here's the amazing thing.

While brokenness is universal, with God redemption is also universal. No matter what cracks and crevices cover our hearts, if we seek the truth of God above all else, He will work all things for good.

Dear Lord, may Your Spirit fall fresh upon me today. Remind me. Reassure me. Rest upon me. Help me to be still and know that You are God. In Jesus' name. Amen.

DAY 20

Disappointment

Take delight in the LORD,
and he will give you the desires of your heart.
(PSALM 37:4)

Thought for the Day:
Disappointment only stings as long as I let it.

The other day a friend asked me if I ever get disappointed. I said yes and threw out a spiritually sound answer. And then the next day happened. The day when a really big disappointment whacked me upside the head and sent my heart sinking. I'd been asked to speak at a really big event — one of the biggest of my life — and then things fell apart.

Invited, thrilled, excited, honored, included turned into uninvited, bummed, sad, disillusioned, left out. And while I still had solid spiritual perspectives to hold on to, my flesh just needed a minute to say, "Stink!"

Because sometimes things do stink. But right when I wanted say

"Stink" a few more times, I spotted a bowl that's been sitting on my dining room table for weeks now. Brooke found some caterpillars awhile back, put them in a bowl, and has been holding them hostage ever since. I mean she's been lovingly admiring them underneath a layer of cellophane.

Wouldn't you know that those caterpillars formed cocoons inside that unlikely environment. And then today, as I was muttering, "Stink!" I glanced across that bowl and sucked the word back down my throat.

The cocoons were empty.

Expecting glorious butterflies, I had to chuckle when I got right over the bowl and closely examined the product of my little girl's hopes for new life.

Moths.

Yet another thing in my day that wasn't quite right.

Or was it?

When Brooke spotted the moths, she was beyond thrilled. Grabbing my hand, she led me outside, ripped off the plastic barrier, and watched the beauty of tiny wings beating ... beating ... beating ... and finally fluttering into flight.

Hmmmm.

As I watched Brooke's sheer delight, I realized she couldn't have cared less if they were moths or butterflies. Creatures that once knew only the dirt of the earth had just been given the gift of flight. Reaching, soaring up, up, and away.

And with that realization, this simple creature pulled up the corners of her mouth into a smile.

Disappointment only stings as long as I let it.

Dear Lord, thank You for Your mercies and patience in this journey of imperfect progress. Forgive me for allowing disappointment to capture my heart so easily. Adjust my perspective and help me to see the things You have brought to life in me. In Jesus' name. Amen.

DAY 21

I Need to Be Honest about My Issues

Search me, God, and know my heart;
test me and know my anxious thoughts.
See if there is any offensive way in me,
and lead me in the way everlasting.

(PSALM 139:23 – 24)

Thought for the Day:
Avoiding reality never changes reality.

Mostly I'm a good person with good motives, but not always. Not when I just want life to be a little more about me or about making sure I look good. That's when my motives get corrupted.

The Bible is pretty blunt in naming the real issue here: evil desires.

Yikes. I don't like that term at all. And it seems a bit severe to call my unglued issues evil desires, doesn't it? But in the depths of my heart I know the truth. Avoiding reality never changes reality. Sigh. I think I should say that again: Avoiding reality never changes reality. And change is what I really want.

So upon the table I now place my honesty: I have evil desires. I do.

Maybe not the kind that will land me on a *48 Hours Mystery* episode, but the kind that pull me away from the woman I want to be. One with a calm spirit and divine nature. I want it to be evident that I know Jesus, love Jesus, and spend time with Jesus each day. So why do other things bubble to the surface when my life gets stressful and my relationships get strained? Things like ...

> *Selfishness:* I want things my way.
>
> *Pride:* I see things only from my vantage point.
>
> *Impatience:* I rush things without proper consideration.
>
> *Anger:* I let simmering frustrations erupt.
>
> *Bitterness:* I swallow eruptions and let them fester.

It's easier to avoid these realities than to deal with them. I'd much rather tidy my closet than tidy my heart. I'd much rather run to the mall and get a new shirt than run to God and get a new attitude. I'd much rather dig into a brownie than dig into my heart. I'd much rather point the finger at other people's issues than take a peek at my own. Plus, it's just a whole lot easier to tidy my closet, run to the store, eat a brownie, and look at other people's issues. A whole lot easier.

I rationalize that I don't have time to get all psychological and examine my selfishness, pride, impatience, anger, and bitterness. And honestly, I'm tired of knowing I have issues but having no clue how to practically rein them in on a given day. I need something simple. A quick reality check I can remember in the midst of the everyday messies.

And I think the following prayer is just the thing:

God, even when I choose to ignore what my heart is saying to me, You know my heart. I bring to You this [and here I name whatever feeling or thoughts I have been reluctant to acknowledge]. *Forgive me. Soften my heart. Make it pure.*

Might that quick prayer help you as well? If so, stop what you are doing—just for five minutes—and pray these or similar words. When I've prayed for the Lord to interrupt my feelings and soften my heart, it's amazing how this changes me.

Dear Lord, help me to remember to actually bring my emotions and reactions to You. I want my heart reaction to be godly. Thank You for grace and for always forgiving me. In Jesus' name. Amen.

DAY 22

Real Problems

Discretion will protect you,
and understanding will guard you.
(PROVERBS 2:11)

Thought for the Day: It's good to know the difference between an inconvenience and a real problem.

I will face issues today that I could think of as problems. I might be tempted to call them problems. They will bother me as if they are problems. I will feel these situations are truly problematic.

But they aren't—not in light of what others are facing today. Real problems. Life-altering problems. Problems that will still sting a month from now, a year from now, ten years from now. My friend Jade battling cancer, hoping to live long enough to see her daughter graduate from high school, is a problem. My daughter forgetting to get a permission slip signed and my having to run up to the school to take care of it is an inconvenience—not a problem.

Indeed, I'll have hard things to face today. I'll have things that make me sad today. I'll have setbacks and interruptions and inconveniences I will deal with today. But not problems.

Oh, that I would know the difference. And when I come to the realization that what I have aren't really problems, I can look at my hard things and see they aren't so hard after all.

I can look at the things that make me sad today and choose to be a little less sad. I can face setbacks without getting set back. I can be interrupted and choose to look for God in the midst of it all. Because I know what real problems are. And what I have aren't those.

I think it's good to know the difference between an inconvenience and a real problem. Don't you?

Dear Lord, thank You for gently leading me toward a perspective change. Help me to recognize the difference between an inconvenience and a real problem. And no matter which one I'm facing, I want to respond according to Your Word. In Jesus' name. Amen.

DAY 23

Vanished

"Do not store up for yourselves treasures on earth, where moths and vermin destroy, and where thieves break in and steal. But store up for yourselves treasures in heaven, where moths and vermin do not destroy, and where thieves do not break in and steal. For where your treasure is, there your heart will be also."

(MATTHEW 6:19–21)

Thought for the Day: Refusing to come unglued is the only way to prove to ourselves it is possible to have a different kind of reaction.

I don't have a lot of nice jewelry. Usually, you'll only find me wearing my wedding ring and another ring Art gave me for our fifteenth wedding anniversary. Other than those two rings, I have only a few simple pieces that have been given to me over the years. Little treasures not worth a lot of money, but special because they hold a lot of memories.

A child's ring my stepdad gave me the day he asked my mom to marry him.

A ring I got for my college graduation.

A bracelet my mom gave me for Christmas several years ago. And another bracelet Art gave me for Valentine's Day this year.

A legacy ring given to me the day my first daughter was born.

My college sorority pin.

A baby's signet ring, with the faint initials of my dad, who left and never came back.

Simple but special.

One day I noticed that the bracelet Art had given me for Valentine's Day wasn't where I thought I left it. I spent several days searching and wondering where I'd put it. Convinced I'd simply misplaced it and would find it soon, I wasn't too worried.

When I still hadn't found it after three days, it dawned on me that maybe I'd put it in a drawer where I keep my other jewelry. I opened the drawer and my heart sank. Everything was gone. The rings. The bracelets. The pin. The one possession I had in this world that connected me to my biological father. Little things that held big memories.

My first reaction was to grab both of my ring fingers. Much to my relief, I'd worn my wedding and anniversary rings. They were safe. But everything else had vanished.

I stared at the open drawer, sat down on a little stool in my bathroom, and willed my tired mind to start making a mental list of reasons to be thankful.

Strange, I know.

Trust me, there were many other lists begging to take up real estate in my brain. Lists of suspects. Lists of memories and how irreplaceable most of the pieces were. Lists of when this might have happened and how. Lists of anything else that might be missing.

Okay, let's be honest, I wanted to come completely unglued and kick into aggressive figure-it-out mode.

But sometimes refusing the pull to come unglued is the only way to prove to ourselves it is possible to have a different kind of reaction. So I willed those other lists aside. After all, I'd already had enough taken from me in that moment. I didn't need to freely hand over my heart as well.

I am thankful for my children who are here and not taken.

I am thankful for my husband who will let me stick my cold feet underneath his legs tonight.

I am thankful for today's sun that shines and the moon whose light will dance with tonight's shadows.

I am thankful for the thousands of steady breaths I take every day and never have to think about.

I am thankful for memories that flicker and ignite on command.

I am thankful to still be able to retrieve those memories.

And on and on I went. Until I could close the drawer and ask God for just one thing. Okay, two things . . .

First, Lord, wrap Your hope around the person who took these things right now and show them another way. They must be in a really bad spot right now. Come near them. And secondly, if possible, might they just return that one thing? Lord, You know what that one thing is. If possible . . . and if not . . . thank You still a thousand times over. For even in the midst of things stolen, I have been given a great gift —remembering all I still have.

When I choose to find things for which to be thankful in the midst of what might otherwise be an emotionally charged moment, it calms me. As I said before, refusing to come unglued is the only way to prove to ourselves it is possible to have a different kind of reaction. How might you refuse the pull of coming unglued today?

Dear Lord, in desperate situations, it's easy for me to come unglued, get aggressive, and try to solve my problems on my own. Instead, I need to freely hand my heart and issues over to You. Help me to focus on my blessing, trust You, and be thankful for what I have. In Jesus' name. Amen.

The Most-Searched-For Answer

"I will instruct you and teach you
in the way you should go;
I will counsel you and watch over you."
(PSALM 32:8)

Thought for the Day: Salvation can't be found in anyone or anything else. There is no other. Only Jesus.

Growing up, I had a plan for how I could make my life good. Get a good education. A good job. A good husband. A few good kids. A good house. A good flower bed out front. And a good minivan parked in the driveway. Then life would be ... good.

Eventually, I had all that good stuff. And I was thankful for it all. I loved my family to pieces. The minivan wasn't all I thought it would be, but I felt like an official mom driving it. So even that wound up being good.

But something inside me still felt hollow. A little off. A little lacking. So, I reasoned, I needed something else to do. Something that would use my gifts and talents. And while these things were fun and satisfying on one level, they too fell short when it came to that deep place ringing with the echoes of empty.

Empty is a heavy load to bear. Wanting to be filled but not knowing what might fill the deep soul leaves a gnawing ache, prompting a search that can seem both futile and shattering at times.

When you try and try, always feeling like the answer is just around the corner, and then it isn't, your heart can split wide open and leak dry all your reserves.

It can make you feel unsatisfied and frustrated with everything. Even those you love. Maybe especially those you love.

So you fake a smile and keep putting one foot in front of the other. But eventually you stop peeking around the next corner hoping the answer is there. Past experience tells you it isn't. And wrapped in that perception is the noose that strangles hope.

Sadly, this is where many women live. I know this place because I lived there. I struggled there. "Salvation is found in no one else, for there is no other name under heaven given to men by which we must be saved" (Acts 4:12). We're not going to find something else to save us — only Jesus is equipped for that job.

No good plan is the answer. Even a good husband, good children, a good friend make a very poor God. No education or job or house can save you.

Salvation can't be found in anyone or anything else. There is no other.

Only Jesus.

And I'm not just talking about claiming to be a Christian. Following the rules and really following Jesus are two totally different things. Going through the motions of religion won't ever satisfy. True satisfaction comes only when we bend low, open our hearts in complete surrender, and say, "Jesus, it's you. Only you. There is no other."

And then we must really live like this is true.

Because it is. True.

Dear Lord, forgive me for trying to fill the empty places of my soul with people, possessions, and positions. I want to know what it means to have You, Lord, as the One who satisfies the deep longings of my heart. Show me. Teach me. Lead me. And I will follow. In Jesus' name. Amen.

DAY 25

Because Sometimes We Forget

In all these things we are more than conquerors
through him who loved us. For I am convinced
that neither death nor life, neither angels nor demons,
neither the present nor the future, nor any powers,
neither height nor depth, nor anything else in all creation,
will be able to separate us from the love of God
that is in Christ Jesus our Lord.

(ROMANS 8:37 – 39)

Thought for the Day:
In Christ, God has given us a new identity.

I know better, but sometimes I feel like God loves me more when I'm keeping my raw emotions in check and less when I'm a little unglued. Do you ever feel that way? Well, God made a powerful statement about Jesus that encourages me in this regard: "This is my Son, whom I love; with him I am well pleased" (Matthew 3:17).

I found a new perspective in this verse when I realized that

Jesus had not yet gone to the cross, performed miracles, or led the masses. God loved His Son and was pleased with Him not based on how He was performing but simply because Jesus is His Son. His Father established and affirmed Jesus' identity before Jesus began His ministry. Jesus heard God, believed God, and remained filled.

In Christ, God has given us a new identity (Romans 6:4). But unlike Christ, we tend to forget who we are. We look to fill our days and our lives with activities and performances, hoping to please others and even God. Our humanity makes us vulnerable and in need of daily reassurance. It's similar to the phenomenon of being satisfied with a large dinner only to wake up the next morning feeling famished. Truth comes in and fills us up. But our cracks, crevices, and circumstances allow the truth to drain right out of us, leaving a hollowness that can haunt.

Therefore, we must stand moment by moment in the reality of our identity before we throw ourselves into any activity. Grasp the truth and rub it deep. Let it sink in quickly and resist the drain of the day's performances. Hear God say, "You are my daughter, whom I love; with you I am well pleased."

Well pleased because of who you are, not because of what you do. Well pleased because of an unfathomable, unconditional love —not earned but simply given.

Lord, thank You for loving me unconditionally. I know Scripture says I am Your daughter and I cannot earn Your love. Please help me walk in my true identity today. In Jesus' name. Amen.

DAY 26

What Frustrated Jesus

I will remember the deeds of the LORD;
yes, I will remember your miracles of long ago.
(PSALM 77:11)

Thought for the Day:
I can be the unglued woman
made gentle, patient, and peaceful.

If I lived in Jesus' day, I would like to think I'd have been moved by
His miracles. Changed by His miracles. Repentant and willing to
live differently because of His miracles. He is the Son of God—the
miracle worker.

But would I really?

After all, sometimes I act as though Jesus can work miracles for
other people, but not for me. Not with my issues.

Last year, my issues with coming unglued and getting all tangled
in my raw emotions constantly left me making promises to do better
tomorrow. But then tomorrow would bring with it more challenges

and conflicts where I'd react and then regret. No, I wasn't sure Jesus could work a miracle with my issues. I was quick to applaud when other people repented and positioned their hearts to see Jesus work a miracle in their lives, but I lived as if that same kind of miracle wasn't possible for me.

This kind of unrepentant attitude frustrates Jesus. Matthew says that Jesus "began to denounce the towns in which most of his miracles had been performed, because they did not repent" (11:20).

Sometimes I have to get out of my normal surroundings to become more aware of things that need to change in me. Last year I spent a week at a homeless shelter called the Dream Center in Los Angeles. Pastor Matthew Barnett and his church run the Dream Center, which is a ministry hub of 120 programs that serve more than 40,000 people every month. Housed in a converted hospital building, the 700-bed facility includes a transitional shelter for homeless families, a drug rehab center, and a shelter for victims of sex trafficking.

I went to help meet needs. But I quickly realized I was there as a woman in need. A woman who needed God's reality to fall fresh and heavy and close and real and too in-my-face to deny.

I saw God's miraculous healing power woven into so many lives at the Dream Center. I saw it, and I wanted it.

God's miraculous power is what transformed the ex–gang member with eight bullet hole scars into a Jesus-loving servant. So gentle.

It's what changed the ex–prostitute into a counselor for other girls rescued from life on the streets. So pure.

It's what changed the ex–drug addict into a loving father, teaching his son how to be a godly leader. So integrity-filled.

What prevented me from realizing that God's power could

change me too? Somewhere along the line I stopped expecting God to work miraculously in me.

Inspired by the changed lives at the homeless shelter, my soul quickened to the bold reality that I could be different. I really could have different reactions to my raw emotions. I knew my progress would be imperfect, but it could still be miraculous. And I felt a new hope rush through me.

I'm not gentle by nature, but I can be gentle by obedience. I'm not patient by nature, but I can be patient by obedience. I'm not peaceful by nature, but I can be peaceful by obedience.

I can. And I will.

I can be the unglued woman made gentle, patient, and peaceful. God, help me. God, forgive me. And in the shadow of that realization and repentance, the miracle begins.

Dear Lord, please open my eyes to see the places I need You to change in me. I know I have wrapped my identity in so many things other than You. I want You to change those rough, imperfect places in my heart. Help me become the woman You created me to be. In Jesus' name. Amen.

Plan for It

Therefore put on the full armor of God,
so that when the day of evil comes,
you may be able to stand your ground,
and after you have done everything, to stand.
(EPHESIANS 6:13)

Thought for the Day: It's God's promises — His truths and examples from Scripture — that are powerful enough to redirect us to the divine nature we're meant to have.

Once, while traveling, I experienced a vivid illustration of how crucial it is to have predetermined procedures. I had taken my seat on a flight to a speaking engagement. Everything seemed to be quite normal during the rest of the boarding process, but as the plane was about to taxi, things got very abnormal. A woman just a few rows behind me started screaming obscenities. And when I say screaming, I don't mean talking too loudly. I mean full-out vocal extremes.

She was completely undone because she found a piece of

chewed gum stuck to her bag of chips. Where the gum came from was a mystery, but how she felt about that gum was not. What came out of her mouth was so R-rated it made my already wide eyes pop out like a bug on steroids.

She was so loud and out of control that the flight attendants quickly alerted the captain to abort the flight. When it became obvious the flight attendants were not going to be able to contain the situation, two plainly dressed men on the plane suddenly stood and flashed federal marshal badges.

One of the marshals gathered the flight crew while the other went to talk to the woman. Every airline professional on board immediately went into by-the-book mode. It was clear they had been well trained on how to handle crazy situations. They didn't get emotional or come unglued in any way. They simply followed procedures. I watched in amazement as the woman kept escalating her wild behavior, but the people trained to handle her never did.

She screamed.

They talked in calm, hushed tones.

She threatened.

They deflected her threats with gentle warnings.

Then she took things to a whole new level: "I have a bomb! I have a bomb! I have a bomb!"

I am not kidding.

I know you think I am. But I am not.

That's when I pulled out the anointing oil my pastor had given to me the day before. My seat became oily and holy. I called Art and my friend Amy and asked them to pray. And I tweeted, asking my cyber friends to pray.

Eventually, the marshals — along with two policemen and additional Homeland Security people who'd boarded the plane —

handcuffed her and removed her from the flight. Throughout the whole hair-raising debacle, I never once heard the people following procedures yell or come unglued even one tiny bit. And I was absolutely amazed.

I will be honest with you: This woman took unglued to a level I hope I never experience again. But I also never want to forget the incredible responses of the flight attendants and officers who dealt with this explosive situation. Not only did their obviously thorough training and procedures keep them calm, they kept an entire planeload of passengers calm as well. And that was an amazing thing to behold.

So, I started thinking that maybe I needed a set of default procedures for when selfishness, pride, impatience, anger, and bitterness rear their ugly heads. Because in the moment I feel them, I feel justified in feeling them and find them hard to battle.

We'll explore my predetermined plan in the next five devotions, but for today, remember it's God's promises — His truths and examples from Scripture — that are powerful enough to redirect us to the divine nature we're meant to have. How do you want to display God's divine nature working in you the next time you feel a little unglued? I want to be calm, levelheaded, and show evidence of loving Jesus. What about you?

Dear Lord, thank You for Your divine power to help me stay out of the emotional fray. Please keep me anchored to the divine nature I am meant to have. In Jesus' name. Amen.

DAY 28

PROCEDURE MANUAL STEP 1:
Remember Who You Are

Alarmed, Jehoshaphat resolved to inquire of the LORD,
and he proclaimed a fast for all Judah.
(2 CHRONICLES 20:3)

Thought for the Day:
Remember who you are.

Raw emotions are hard to battle in the heat of the moment, so I started thinking I should have a set of default procedures to follow when selfishness, pride, impatience, anger, and bitterness rear their ugly heads. And I found a great example of what I was looking for in an Old Testament king named Jehoshaphat (2 Chronicles 20).

Jehoshaphat was in an overwhelming situation. Three countries had banded together, forming a massive army to attack his much smaller country of Judah. If ever there were a time for a king to feel unglued, this would have been it. But Jehoshaphat didn't fall apart. And I think a big reason he didn't come unglued is explained by this three-word sentence: "*Alarmed*, Jehoshaphat *resolved*" (2 Chronicles 20:3, emphasis added).

The king had *resolved* to inquire of the Lord. This is how I want to be. When I feel alarmed, I want to simultaneously be resolved. *Alarmed*, Lysa *resolved*. And here's what I want to be resolved to do —to remember who I am.

We have a four-word family motto we say to our kids almost every time they step out the door of our home. These four words encapsulate every moral lesson, every biblical lesson, and every life lesson we've taught them. Instead of blasting them with a sermonette— "Be nice, use your manners, watch your words, don't drink, don't smoke, and don't drive over the speed limit" — all we give them are four words:

Remember who you are.

"Remember, you are a TerKeurst, and a good name is better than all the riches of the world. And even more important than that, remember you are a child of God, holy and dearly loved, whom God has set apart for a mighty plan."

King Jehoshaphat was resolved. He predetermined to remember who he was. And it prevented him from coming unglued. I need to do the very same thing. I'm not an unglued woman who is a slave to her circumstances, her hormones, or other people's attitudes. Those things might affect me, but they don't rule me. I am a child of God, holy and dearly loved, whom He has set apart for a mighty plan. And there ain't nothing in this world worth trading all that for. Indeed, I must remember who I am.

Dear Lord, today I want to remember I am a child of God, holy and dearly loved. You've set me apart for a mighty plan. Please help me remember these things as I try to serve and live for You. In Jesus' name. Amen.

DAY 29

PROCEDURE MANUAL STEP 2:
There Is Power in the Name

We do not know what to do,
but our eyes are on you.
(2 CHRONICLES 20:12)

Thought for the Day:
There is power and protection in the Lord's name.

Yesterday, we talked about being alarmed but also resolved. What do we do next?

Isn't it frustrating to be in situations, conflicts, hard places, and have no idea what to do—to feel as if there are no easy solutions and no certain answers? But I love the honest admission by King Jehoshaphat and his people. They didn't know what to do, but they knew *who* to turn to. Their attention was fixed on the Lord. I have relied on the truth of 2 Chronicles 20:12 many times over when I didn't know what to do.

A few years ago, I was nearing the end of a conference at which I'd been speaking, and looking forward to a relaxing dinner with our team that night. My friend Beth and I were talking about potential restaurant choices when a frantic arena staff member told us there was an emergency and we were needed right away. A woman attending the conference had just been told her two grandchildren had been killed that day in a fire. Moments later we were at the side of a woman lying on the floor, surrounded by her friends, and sobbing to the point she could hardly breathe.

The woman's grandbabies, ages eight and four, had recently spent spring break with her. Just days earlier, she'd held them, rocked them, stroked their hair, and kissed them all over their faces. How could they be gone? The tragic news was too much for her to process, and she'd collapsed.

The EMT who'd been trying to help her breathe stepped aside so we could hold the woman's hands and pray with her. At first, I stumbled my way through requests for Jesus to pour His most tender mercies into this situation. I prayed for comfort and the reassurance that these precious children were being held by Jesus at that moment. It was so hard. My mommy heart ached deeply for this woman, and I couldn't contain my own tears.

As my friend Beth began to pray, I noticed something miraculous. Every time she said "Jesus," the woman's body relaxed, her crying slowed, and her breathing eased. So when it was my turn to pray again, I just said His name over and over and over. This sweet grandmother joined me, "Jesus, Jesus, Jesus."

As we continued to repeat the name of Jesus, we felt an outpouring of power beyond what we were capable of mustering up on our own. The Bible teaches that there is power and protection in the Lord's name (John 17:11). I saw that power. I experienced it. And

I won't soon forget it. That's why whispering the name of Jesus is definitely part of my procedure manual for raw reactions. Whether we are facing an emergency situation or an everyday unglued reaction, the name of Jesus brings peace.

The human soul is designed to recognize and respond to the calm assurance of Jesus. When I am in an unglued place, I can invite a power beyond my own into the situation simply by speaking His name. I don't have to know what to do. I don't have to have all the answers. I don't have to remember everything I learned in Bible study last week. I just have to remember one thing, one name —Jesus.

Dear Lord, thank You for being my source of help when I am in trouble. I need Your power and protection daily. Help me remember to come running to You. In Jesus' precious name. Amen.

DAY 30

PROCEDURE MANUAL STEP 3:
Walking in the Flow

He said: "Listen, King Jehoshaphat
and all who live in Judah and Jerusalem!
This is what the LORD says to you:
'Do not be afraid or discouraged because of this vast army.
For the battle is not yours, but God's.'"

(2 CHRONICLES 20:15)

Thought for the Day: Seeking to obey God in the midst of whatever circumstance I'm facing is what positions me in the flow of God's power.

Tucked away in the Adirondack Mountains of New York, Camp-of-the-Woods is an amazing getaway for families — great chapel preaching every morning, no TV, crystal-clear lake, campfires, fishing, putt-putt golf, shuffleboard, and more game playing than you can imagine. It's also an incredibly beautiful place with all kinds of scenic views and walking trails. So when some exercise-loving friends suggested we join them for a moderate family hike, we thought that was a great idea.

Well, it turns out their definition of *moderate* came from an entirely different dictionary than mine. Actually, an entirely different planet, if I'm being completely honest. Honey, honey, honey … this was no *moderate* hike.

I had pictured a path with a gently winding, upward slope. But what we actually experienced was more like scaling a cliff face made entirely of rocks and roots.

Not kidding.

And we were at an altitude so high my lungs felt like they were stuck together and incapable of holding more than a thimbleful of breath. Lovely. And forget having any type of conversation. All I could do was mutter a few moans between my gasps for air.

Up, up, up we went. And when another group of hikers passed us on their way down and cheerfully quipped, "You're almost halfway there!" I wanted to quit. *Halfway?* How could we be only halfway?!

I pushed. I pulled. I strained. I huffed and puffed. And I might have even spent a few minutes pouting. But eventually, we reached the top. I bent over, holding my sides and wondering how a girl who runs four miles almost every day of her life could feel so stinkin' out of shape!

Climbing up the mountain against the force of gravity was hard. Really, really hard. But coming down was a completely different experience. I navigated the same rocks and roots without feeling nearly as stressed. I enjoyed the journey. I noticed more of the beautiful surroundings and had enough breath to actually talk all the way down.

About halfway down the trail, it occurred to me how similar my experience of this hike was to my Christian walk. Starting at the top of the mountain and working *with* the force of gravity was so much easier than starting at the bottom of the mountain and working *against* it. Although I had to navigate the exact same path both directions, being in the flow of gravity made the journey so much better.

It's just like when I face a hard issue in life. Operating *in the flow* of God's power is so much better than working *against the flow* of God's power. Seeking to obey God in the midst of whatever circumstance I'm facing is what positions me to work in the flow of God's power. I still have to navigate the realities of my situation, but I won't be doing it in my own strength. My job is to be obedient to God, to apply His Word, and to walk according to His ways — not according to the world's suggestions. God, in His way and timing, works it all out.

That's what happened with King Jehoshaphat in 2 Chronicles 20. He stayed in the flow of obeying God in his actions and reactions. I'm sure if he had tried to figure out how to win this battle based on his limited strength and numbers alone, he would have surely given up. Judah was outnumbered. No question. But instead of counting themselves out, the king and his army counted God in and determined to do exactly as He instructed.

I want to participate in God's divine nature rather than wallow in my own bad attitude and insecurities. Then I won't have to huff and puff and pout while trying to figure everything out on my own.

I stay in the flow.

Lord, help me to trust that You've got it all figured out and to remember that I don't. Help me to say yes to You even when it's hard. Help me to say no to anything that doesn't align with Your Word. Amen.

DAY 31

PROCEDURE MANUAL STEP 4:
Attitude of Gratitude

*After consulting the people, Jehoshaphat appointed men
to sing to the LORD and to praise him for the splendor
of his holiness as they went out at the head of the army, saying:
"Give thanks to the LORD, for his love endures forever."*
(2 CHRONICLES 20:21)

Thought for the Day: If this is the worst thing that happens to me today, it's still a pretty good day.

I don't know about you, but if I had been facing certain death at the hands of a marauding horde, my first line of defense would not have been to send out the choir. Reread today's key verse and let King Jehoshaphat's obedient decision really sink in.

Oh, if only I were more in the habit of having a thankful heart full of praises instead of a grumbling heart consumed with circumstances. The hard thing is, I don't feel very thankful in that moment when problems start bumping into my happy. I just don't feel like busting out in a praise song. I wish I did. But I don't.

So in the midst of an unglued moment, how do I shift from *having an attitude* to *walking in gratitude*? I need a go-to script that will redirect my perspective to a better place. And I think I have just the thing. I say out loud to myself, "If this is the worst thing that happens to me today, it's still a pretty good day."

My friend just hurt my feelings. If this is the worst thing that happens to me today, it's still a pretty good day. Praise You, God.

My husband is running late getting home from work, and now I have to stay with the kids and miss the fun girls' night out I'd been planning to attend. If this is the worst thing that happens to me today, it's still a pretty good day. Praise You, God.

My Bible study leader just asked Stacey to fill in for her next week when I've often told her, "I'd love to do that sometime." If this is the worst thing that happens to me today, it's still a pretty good day. Praise You, God.

I can't authentically praise God for anything that is wrong or evil, but I sure can shift my focus to all that is right and praise Him for that. And in the story of King Jehoshaphat, making this shift —from looking at what was wrong to praising God for what was right—worked a miracle.

When the praise chorus from Judah's front line of defense reached the ears of the opposing armies, these enemies were so confused that rather than fight against Judah, they started fighting among themselves instead. And "when the men of Judah came to the place that overlooks the desert and looked toward the vast army, they saw only dead bodies lying on the ground; no one had escaped" (2 Chronicles 20:24). Amazing! Absolutely amazing.

Oh, how powerful it is to shift from an attitude to gratitude and to praise our God in the midst of it all. When I do this, my circumstances may not instantly change, but the way I look at those circumstances certainly does. I stop being blind to all that's right and see so many more reasons to praise God. And when my heart is full of praise, my emotions aren't nearly as prone to coming unglued!

Dear Lord, I'm challenged in the best of ways to shift my focus from what is wrong to all that is right and praise You for that. Thanks for Your help! In Jesus' name. Amen.

DAY 32

PROCEDURE MANUAL STEP 5:
Your Reactions Determine
Your Reach

The fear of God came on all the surrounding kingdoms
when they heard how the LORD had fought against the enemies
of Israel. And the kingdom of Jehoshaphat was at peace,
for his God had given him rest on every side.
(2 CHRONICLES 20:29 – 30)

Thought for the Day: My reactions testify to the kind of relationship
I have with Jesus and the kind of effect He has on my heart.

We've covered the first four steps of the procedure manual, and
today we're covering the most important step of all: Your reactions
determine your reach. Each step we've covered so far builds to this
fifth step. Remember what we've learned:

- Though Jehoshaphat was alarmed, he was resolved to inquire
  of the Lord. He felt alarmed but stayed resolved.

101

- He kept his focus on the Lord.

- He stayed in the flow of God's power by being obedient to God's Word.

- It wasn't easy, but Jehoshaphat shifted from having an attitude to practicing gratitude.

Because Jehoshaphat did each of those things, his reaction positively affected everyone around him, not only in his own kingdom but in surrounding countries. This is the kind of leader I want to follow. This is the kind of leader I want to be. Not that I'm leading a kingdom, but I *am* influencing the people around me.

The interactions I have with my kids, my husband, my friends, my neighbors, my church, even the checkout clerk at my local grocery store—they matter. My reactions testify to the relationship I have with Jesus and the effect He has on my heart. After all, I'm reminded in the Bible that out of the overflow of the heart the mouth speaks. When my happy gets bumped, what's really going on in my heart is on display. In those times I will either add to the authenticity of my love for Jesus or, sadly, negate it.

Yes, my reactions determine my reach. That's why when I feel the great unglued coming on, I want to train my mind to remember each step, each truth, each choice Jehoshaphat made. Then I want to train my heart to have the courage to implement each one.

So here's the short version of my predetermined biblical procedure manual all in one place:

1. Alarmed, I resolve to remember who I am.

2. Jesus, Jesus, Jesus.

3. Stay in the flow—my job is obedience; God's job is results.

4. Shift from an attitude to gratitude.

5. My reactions determine my reach.

Instead of avoiding the fact that I come unglued, I'm tackling it head-on. I want to give myself every fighting chance to make wise choices in the midst of raw emotions. And a predetermined plan is a good thing to create and implement. Care to join me? Not that your plan will look the same as mine. Feel free to take this idea and make it your own. The best kind of plan for you is the one you'll follow.

Dear Lord, in times when my happy gets bumped, help me to add to the authenticity of my love for You, not negate it. In Jesus' name. Amen.

DAY 33

I'm Really Afraid!

The angel of the LORD
encamps around those who fear him,
and he delivers them.

(PSALM 34:7)

Thought for the Day: When you know the Lord is with you, you can face your fears without coming unglued.

Last year, one of my back teeth started hurting — again. And quite honestly, I just didn't want to deal with it. This tooth had been a complete pain. Literally.

I'd had not one, not two, but *three* crowns done on the same tooth. The first one broke. The second one broke. And although it initially seemed the third one would finally work, the tooth started aching again. Ugggh.

The dentist informed me that the only thing to do at this point was to have a root canal. I'm okay with the word *root*. And I'm okay with the word *canal*. But when he put those two words together, a wild fear whipped its tentacles around my heart and squeezed the life right out of me. I couldn't do it. I just couldn't bring myself to schedule the procedure.

So I dealt with the throbbing pain. For a whole year, I didn't chew on that side of my mouth. I didn't let cold drinks leak over to that side. And I took ibuprofen when the throbbing got the best of me. *A year!*

When the pain grew bigger than my fear, I'd finally had enough and made the appointment for the dreaded root canal.

And you know what? I survived! Not only did I survive, but I honestly found the whole root canal ordeal to be no big deal. The fear of it was so much worse than actually having the procedure.

Fear often plays out that way. Many times, living in fear of what might be causes more stress and anxiety than actually facing what we fear.

I love this reassuring promise: "The angel of the LORD encamps around those who fear him, and he delivers them" (Psalm 34:7). To fear the Lord means to honor Him and magnify Him most of all in my heart. When I magnify my fears instead, they become all I can think about. So I've learned to focus on God by doing three things:

1. I cry out to Him with honest prayers. I verbalize to God what I'm afraid of and how paralyzing my fear is. I ask Him to help me see each next step I need to take.

2. I open my Bible and look for verses that show me what He wants me to do in that moment of fear. I write down biblical truths about fear and then align my next steps with His truth.

3. I walk in the assurance that I am fearing (or honoring) the Lord, and therefore I know with certainty that an angel of the Lord is encamped around me and God will deliver me.

I love this promise so much—it comforts me, reassures me, and challenges me to live like I really believe it's true.

Is there something you've been avoiding because you're afraid? An everyday fear that's holding you back? Perhaps it's initiating a really hard conversation that needs to happen with a friend or family member, or owning up to an explosive reaction that occurred in a moment of unglued panic, or dealing with a medical diagnosis you just received. Maybe you're fearful of a root canal.

When you feel fear, focus on God by crying out to Him in prayer. Align your reactions with His truth. Then pray with the reassurance of His presence. When you know the Lord is with you, you can face your fears without coming unglued.

Dear Lord, help me to fear only You. If a feeling of fear is a legitimate warning from You, help me to know that. But if this feeling of fear is a distraction, help me be courageous and walk in the confident assurance of Your presence. In Jesus' name. Amen.

DAY 34

Weak Places, Strong Places

The Spirit helps us in our weakness.
We do not know what we ought to pray for,
but the Spirit himself intercedes for us
with groans that words cannot express.

(ROMANS 8:26)

Thought for the Day:
With the power of Christ,
all things can be made new.

We all have them. Weak places. Places inside us that make us wonder if we'll ever get it together like the together people. Places that make us feel less than — less than victorious, less than a conqueror, less than strong.

My weak places frustrate me. And yet I refuse to believe they can't ever be changed. With the power of Christ, all things can be made new and all broken things can be restored. But sometimes I get so tired of feeling weak.

Weak places are like the lever that flips open the drain in my bathtub. My whole world can feel full and warm and clean until that little lever is pulled. Suddenly, the warm comfort is sucked away, leaving me shivering in a cold, hard, residue-filled space. Cold, hard, and residue-filled is exactly what those weak places make me feel inside.

What is your weak place? A temper that flares? An insecurity that stings? A family dysfunction that is always brewing?

May I breathe a little life into your weakness today? Whatever it is, however large it may loom, know that "the Spirit helps us in our weakness. We do not know what we ought to pray for, but the Spirit himself intercedes for us with groans that words cannot express" (Romans 8:26).

We don't have to have all the answers. We don't have to make suggestions to God. It's okay to be so tired of our weak places that we run out of words to pray.

Listen to the beautiful verses tucked all around this verse about weak places:

There is no condemnation for those who are in Christ Jesus. (Romans 8:1)

You, however, are not controlled by the sinful nature but by the Spirit. (Romans 8:9)

If God is for us, who can be against us? (Romans 8:31)

No, in all these things we are more than conquerors through him who loved us. (Romans 8:37)

Maybe we need to sit still for just a moment or two today. Quiet, without the weight of condemnation or the swirl of trying to figure things out. Quiet, with nothing but the absolute assurance that the Spirit helps us in our weakness.

He knows what to pray. He understands our weak places. There is a purpose to this weak place. Though it doesn't feel good, we can trust that good will come from it (Romans 8:28).

In that quiet stillness, while the Spirit prays for us and we just simply soak in truth, there will be a flicker of light. A slight trickle of hope. A grace so unimaginable, we'll feel His power overshadowing our weakness. Even the smallest drop of God's strength is more than enough to cover our frailties, our shortcomings, the places where we deem ourselves weak.

And we'll reject that label — we aren't weak.

We are dependent. Dependent on the only One powerful enough to help us. The only One sufficient enough to cover us in grace throughout the process of growing stronger.

Our relationships may not be sufficient. Our circumstances may not be sufficient. Our willpower may not be sufficient. Our confidence may not be sufficient. But God is sufficient — and forever will be.

Hear Him speak this promise straight to your heart: "My grace is sufficient for you, for my power is made perfect in weakness" (2 Corinthians 12:9).

So instead of wallowing in my weak place, I will let the Spirit reveal the one positive step I can take today. I will wash away the condemnation with the warmth of His grace. I will receive His power. And I will rename the weakness my strong place. "For when I am weak, then I am strong" (2 Corinthians 12:10).

Dear Lord, I am so grateful that when I am weak, You are strong. Help me to see positive steps I can take to grow stronger in my weak places. In Jesus' name. Amen.

DAY 35

Where Is God?

*Then God opened her eyes
and she saw a well of water.*

(GENESIS 21:19)

Thought for the Day:
God isn't trying to hide from us. He's waiting for us to see Him.

I am asked lots of questions when I meet people at conferences.

Practical questions ... "How did you get started speaking and writing?"

Hilarious questions ... "Why do you look so much better in person than in the photos on your books?"

Heart-wrenching questions ... "How did you forgive the people who hurt you so much?"

Hard questions ... "Why would God let this happen?"

Honest questions ... "How can I find God, connect with God, in the midst of my everyday life?"

It's that last question that compels me to do what I do. It's what makes me sit at the computer and tangle with words and truths and vulnerable admissions. It's what compels me to split my heart wide open and let people see the not-so-great stuff about me mixed in with all the gracious goodness of God.

Because if I can help a soul find an authentic, honest way to connect with God, all the other questions will settle down a bit, wait more patiently, maybe decide it's okay if they go unanswered.

Except for the question about my photos. Some people have the "it" factor in photos and some don't. It doesn't matter how many times I get my pictures done, I still get the same comment. Everywhere. I. Go. Without. Exception. Heaven. Help. Me.

Anyhow.

Connection with God is such a deeply personal and uniquely individual process. Surely it can't be reduced to three points and a poem. But there are two words that stir me. Move me. Propel me. Two words I hear Jesus saying over and over: "Follow Me."

Tucked within these two words, three syllables, eight letters is the wild secret of deep connection with God.

If we want to know God, we have to follow Him.

Follow His instructions.

Follow His heart.

Follow His example.

Not just follow along as we mindlessly repeat the words of Jesus songs and scribble some notes during the pastor's sermon.

No.

Really follow. Follow hard. Follow passionately. Follow fully. Follow with engaged minds and willing hearts and open hands and ready feet.

And where can we start this kind of all-out following?

By asking God to let us see Him.

When we pray, we invite the divine presence of the almighty God to do life with us that day. Then we need to watch for Him —go on a God-hunt and make connections between the things we pray for and the things that happen throughout the day. This is the direct evidence of His hand at work—in us, around us, and in spite of us.

Rest assured, God isn't trying to hide from us. He is waiting for us to see Him.

Dear Lord, You are so good—faithful, fulfilling, encouraging, and worthy of following with all my heart, mind, and soul. I invite You into my day. Help me to keep my eyes open and to recognize Your hand at work in my life. In Jesus' name. Amen.

DAY 36

Getting Unstuck
from My Thinking Rut

Do not conform any longer to the pattern of this world,
but be transformed by the renewing of your mind.
Then you will be able to test and approve what God's will is —
his good, pleasing and perfect will.

(ROMANS 12:2)

Thought for the Day:
We won't develop new responses
until we develop new thoughts.

Brain research shows that every conscious thought we have is recorded on our internal hard drive known as the cerebral cortex. Each thought scratches the surface much like an Etch A Sketch. When we have the same thought again, the line of the original thought is deepened, causing what's called a memory trace. With each repetition the trace goes deeper and deeper, forming and embedding a pattern of thought. When an emotion is tied to this thought pattern, the memory trace grows exponentially stronger.

We forget most of our random thoughts that are not tied to an emotion. However, we retain the ones we think often that have an emotion tied to them. For example, if we've had the thought over and over that we are "unglued," and that thought is tied to a strong emotion, we deepen the memory trace when we repeatedly access that thought. The same is true if we decide to stuff a thought—we'll perpetuate that stuffing. Or if we yell, we'll keep yelling.

We won't develop new responses until we develop new thoughts. That's why renewing our minds with new thoughts is crucial. New thoughts come from new perspectives. The Bible encourages this process, which only makes sense because God created the human mind and understands better than anyone how it functions.

A foundational teaching of Scripture is that it is possible to be completely changed through transformed thought patterns. That's exactly the point of today's key Scripture. Scripture also teaches that we can accept or refuse thoughts. Instead of being held hostage by old thought patterns, we can actually capture our thoughts and allow the power of Christ's truth to change them:

> We demolish arguments and every pretension that sets itself up against the knowledge of God, and we take captive every thought to make it obedient to Christ. (2 Corinthians 10:5)

I don't know about you, but understanding how my brain is designed makes these verses come alive in a whole new way for me. Taking thoughts captive and being transformed by thinking in new ways isn't some New Age form of mind control. It's biblical, and it's fitting with how God wired our brains.

I can't control the things that happen to me each day, but I can control how I think about them. I can say to myself, "I have a choice to have destructive thoughts or constructive thoughts right now. I can wallow in what's wrong and make things worse, or I can ask God for a better perspective to help me *see* good even when I don't *feel* good." Indeed, when we gain new perspectives, we can see new ways of thinking. And if we change the way we think, we'll change the ways we act and react.

Jesus, teach me to trust You and to believe that even though my situation is overwhelming, You are out to do me good. Give me Your perspective today. Amen.

DAY 37

Move Over, Mean Girl

Then Jesus said to his disciples,
"Whoever wants to be my disciple must deny themselves
and take up their cross and follow me."
(MATTHEW 16:24)

Thought for the Day: It's amazing how quickly my "mean girl" vanishes when I deny myself, admit my own sin, and choose to let Jesus interrupt me.

Last year, we logged over twenty hours in the car during the joy-filled excursion called *family vacation*. It was family bonding at its finest. Here's a little glimpse of the sweet conversations that could be heard coming from the backseat.

Ashley: "Mom, Brooke just licked my hash brown! Ewwwwww!"

Me: "Brooke, why would you lick your sister's hash brown, for heaven's sake?"

Brooke: "Because my arm hurts."

Me: "Oh. Well, that just makes complete sense."

Okay, that's just one exchange. And then there may have been 127 other instances when the soundtrack of my car-traveling life was, "Mom... she poked me, and she's on my side, and she just spilled her drink, and she took my iPod."

And on occasion, I may have wanted to jump in the backseat and remove every shred of candy from my little tweenager people's hands and dump it out the window. But I really didn't want my mean girl or my mean mommy to come out on the family vacation, y'all.

What does Jesus say about this?

He says we must do three things. Not three easy steps but three shifts of the heart. We have to deny ourselves, take up our cross, and follow Him (Matthew 16:24).

Deny myself... I have to deny myself the momentary satisfaction of the quick comeback, the rude response, or the full-out yelling. Oversugared children can elicit craziness in a mama. Not that I have any personal experience with such things. No, not at all. And if you believe that, I've got some Easter candy off on the side of the road somewhere I could sell you.

Deny myself. It's hard. But it is the way with Jesus.

Then I must take up my cross ... *my* cross. Stop the blaming and finger pointing and wishing everyone else would change and start seeing my sinful reaction as a contribution to the problem at hand. I must take my issues to His cross and see my sin for what it is—sin. And I must be disgusted enough by my sin to truly want to do something about it.

Take up my cross. It's hard. But it is the way with Jesus.

Finally, I must follow Him ... really follow Him. Follow *who* He is and *how* He is. I must close my mouth, pause long enough to let Him interrupt my eruption, and let His Spirit redirect me.

Yes, my children need to be corrected, but I can let the consequences scream so I don't have to. Only a calm mama can think of rational, reasonable consequences that instruct.

Follow who He is and how He is. It's hard. But it is the way with Jesus.

It's amazing how quickly my mean girl vanishes when I deny myself, admit my sin, and choose to let Jesus interrupt me.

Just don't be licking my hash brown if your arm starts hurting, okay? I have to draw the line somewhere.

Dear Lord, I don't want my mean girl to come out when I'm angered or aggravated. Give me the self-control to deny myself, stop blaming others, and choose to follow You. Amen.

DAY 38

Gentleness Is in Me

Let your gentleness be evident to all.
(PHILIPPIANS 4:5)

Thought for the Day: The more I rejoice, the more I keep things in perspective. The more I keep things in perspective, the gentler I become.

Lately, I've had this Bible verse chasing me around: "Let your gentleness be evident to all" (Philippians 4:5). I've run across this verse in so many unexpected places that I know it's something God wants me to pay attention to. Why? Let's just say, when the Lord was handing out the gentleness gene in July of 1969, I was apparently in another line waiting for something else. Lots of people who were being fashioned at the same time did get the gentleness gene. I know some people who I'm sure stood in line twice and got a double portion. Me? Not so much.

Now, I can have moments of gentleness. I can perform acts of gentleness. But gentleness doesn't ooze from the core of who I am.

This is especially true if I am sleepy or stressed. Honestly, I think I need one of those warning signs on the bedroom door to enter at your own risk after 8:30 p.m.: "DANGER! Please note that the Holy Spirit has temporarily left this woman's body to go help a sister halfway around the world who is just now waking up."

Now, I know that is some terrible theology, but I'm being honest, y'all. What little threads of gentleness I do have are not evident past 8:30 p.m. Not. At. All.

And then there is this thing that happens when I get stressed. Normally, I can pull off a little gentleness throughout the day, but throw in a stressful situation where too much is coming at me too quickly and mercy lou! I get task-oriented and start talking in a staccato-like cadence to my people, because I want the stuff around the house done. right. now. not. in. ten. minutes. because. now. means. now!

I don't want this to be how my kids remember me. Staccato mama.

I don't want this to be how *I* remember me in this season of life.

So this Philippians verse that has been nipping at the edges of my heart and mind, about letting my gentleness be evident to all, is something I know I need — even if it does sting a bit.

Here's a little sermon I've been preaching to myself: Let *your* gentleness be evident to all. The "your" part means I do have some. Much as I'd like to believe otherwise, God didn't skip over me in distributing the gentleness gene, and my wildfire personality isn't a divine exception. Regardless of the stress I'm under, I am capable of displaying God's gentleness because the Holy Spirit is in me. I have the Holy Spirit in me when I feel all chipper at 8:30 a.m., and I have the Holy Spirit in me when I feel grumpy at 8:30 p.m. The Spirit is in me when I feel calm and when I feel stressed. Gentleness is in *me*!

I just have to learn to reclaim the gentleness that is rightfully mine. And I can reclaim it by practicing the one word that appears right before "Let your gentleness be evident to all" (Philippians 4:5). That little word is *rejoice*: "Rejoice in the Lord always. I will say it again: Rejoice!" (Philippians 4:4). The more my heart is parked in a place of thanksgiving and rejoicing, the less room I have for grumpiness.

My kids are driving me crazy? At least they are healthy enough to have that kind of energy. Don't miss this chance to rejoice.

My laundry is piled to the ceiling? Every stitch of clothing is evidence of life in my home. Don't miss this chance to rejoice.

My husband isn't all skippy romantic about the two of us shopping together? In the grand scheme of life, so what? He's a good man. Don't miss this chance to rejoice.

I feel unorganized and behind and late on everything? Scale back, let unrealistic expectations go, and savor some happy moments today. Don't miss this chance to rejoice.

The more I rejoice, the more I keep things in perspective. The more I keep things in perspective, the gentler I become.

That's why I have to intentionally seek out perspective-magnifying opportunities. Things like serving at a soup kitchen, delivering gifts to a family in need, or going on a mission trip. If I want the gentleness inside me to be unleashed, I have to break away from my everyday routine. I have to go where perspective awaits me.

Dear Lord, some days I just don't feel gentle. But I do want to obey Your Word. So right now, I ask You to help me change my perspective and walk in the gentleness You have given me. In Jesus' name. Amen.

DAY 39

He's for You,
but Are You for God?

What, then, shall we say in response to this?
If God is for us, who can be against us?
(ROMANS 8:31)

Thought for the Day:
I can face things out of my control
without acting out of control.

If ever there were a moment for someone to feel overwhelmed at facing a situation totally out of his control, Joshua's experience outside the wall of Jericho would have been it. He had a battle plan, but it was crazy. God told Joshua that this wall of impossibility would fall if Joshua's troops would march around it a certain number of times on a certain number of days, toot their horns, and yell out a big yee-haw. Well, I don't know for certain that's what they were supposed to yell, but if they were southern Israelites like me, chances are it was something like that. Regardless, short of a miraculous intervention from God, it wouldn't work. Joshua would be shamed. His people would be defeated. And to those who didn't believe, the God of Israel would be revealed as nothing more than a figment of Joshua's overactive imagination.

Talk about pressure.

This is all part of the story with which you're probably familiar. But there's a crucial part of this story that many people miss. It's at the end of Joshua 5 when Joshua goes out to look at the wall before receiving his marching orders from the Lord.

There he is. And there the wall is.

Despite Joshua's long military experience, he had never led an attack on a city that was so well prepared for a long siege. In fact, of all the walled cities in Canaan, Jericho was probably the most invincible. There was also the question of armaments. Israel's army had no siege engines, no battering rams, and no catapults. Their only weapons were slingshots, arrows, and spears — which were like straw toys against the walls of Jericho. Yet Joshua knew the battle of Jericho must be won because, having crossed the Jordan River, Israel's troops had no place to which they could retreat. Further, they could not bypass the city because that would leave their women, children, animals, and goods at Gilgal vulnerable to certain destruction.

Pondering these heavy thoughts, Joshua is suddenly confronted by a man with a drawn sword. Scripture reveals that this is no mere human (Joshua 5:14). This is the commander of the Lord's army — God's presence in human form. Seeing that the man is ready for battle, Joshua asks, "Are you for us or for our enemies?" (Joshua 5:13).

Wrapped in this honest question we see hesitancy in Joshua — a peek inside his thought life — a need for reassurance. Such an honest question, but one that makes me feel Joshua isn't walking in complete confidence and assurance. If he were, he wouldn't have asked. But he did. And this is where we assume that of course God's presence will answer, "Joshua, I am with you, for you, and on your side!"

But we would assume wrong.

When asked, "Are you for us or for our enemies?" the presence of God says, "Neither."

Why?

Because Joshua has asked the wrong question of the wrong person. The question that needed to be asked and answered wasn't whose side God was on. The real question was one Joshua should have asked himself:

"Whose side am *I* on?"

The same goes for us. When faced with a situation out of our control, we need to ask, "Whose side am I on?" Will our response reflect that we are on God's side or not? If we determine that no matter what we're on God's side, it settles the trust issue in our hearts. And if we ground ourselves in the reality that we trust God, we can face circumstances that are out of our control without acting out of control. We can't always fix our circumstances, but we can fix our minds on God. We can do that.

Joshua did it. Joshua obeyed God completely. With that, the walls of Jericho came crashing down. They were impossible no more.

I like the thought of *impossible* being erased from my vocabulary. Especially when it comes to my struggles with feeling unglued. I am on God's side. I can reflect that in my actions and reactions.

I can face things out of my control without acting out of control.
Amen? Amen.

God, thank You for the example of Joshua. With Your help, I know I can face things out of my control with grace and truth. Please help me to settle the trust issues in my heart. Amen.

DAY 40

Coming Unglued Isn't All Bad

Therefore do not let sin reign in your mortal body
so that you obey its evil desires. Do not offer the parts
of your body to sin, as instruments of wickedness,
but rather offer yourselves to God, as those who have been
brought from death to life; and offer the parts of your body
to him as instruments of righteousness.

(ROMANS 6:12 – 13)

Thought for the Day: Coming unglued is glorious if the end result
of that brokenness leads us to a healthier wholeness.

A well-decorated home isn't a sign of a well-built house. It may
seem impressive temporarily, but in the long run, if the foundation
crumbles or faulty wiring makes it catch on fire, it won't matter how
many pretty pictures are on the walls. The whole house will fall.

The same is true of what we might call a well-decorated life.
I can fake a smile, but if I'm crumbling underneath, eventually I
will fall.

My crumbling comes in the form of feeling short-tempered, on edge emotionally, and incapable of explaining exactly what's wrong. My falling comes at the times when those festering feelings bubble to the surface in the form of unglued reactions.

But just as a light that fails to come on when the switch is flipped may indicate a wiring problem, coming unglued may indicate a problem with our internal wiring. Outward expressions indicate internal realities. If our outward expression is unglued, we are experiencing brokenness internally — brokenness we won't address unless we are forced to acknowledge its existence. As painful as it might be to name these broken places, seeing ourselves — really seeing deeply and honestly — is a good thing.

When I look through the window of my unglued reactions, I may find unacknowledged pride, long-standing unforgiveness, deep-seated bitterness, simmering anger, joy-stealing jealousy, condemning shame, haunting regrets, and entangling rejection. Or I might see a crammed-too-full schedule. Or a feeling that I'm taken for granted and unappreciated.

Romans 6:12 reminds us not to let sin reign in us; therefore, we have to be aware of the sin inside. If things are ever going to get better, we have to acknowledge things under the surface that fuel our unglued reactions. We may not like what we see, but at least we'll know what we're dealing with. We can call it what it is and ask God to help us.

I'm reacting in angry ways, God. What do I do?
I'm feeling bitter toward them, God. What do I do?
I'm having a hard time forgiving, God. What do I do?
I'm using harsh words, God. What do I do?

I don't take time to ask God what to do often enough. Do you find this to be true? So maybe having a clear-eyed view of my underneath will help me to go to God more — more frequently, more authentically, more humbly.

Therefore, might we agree that coming unglued isn't all bad if it brings us to God? And brings to light what's eating away at us, what's chipping away at our foundation? But even more, coming unglued is glorious if the end result of that brokenness leads us to a healthier wholeness.

Dear Lord, open my heart and eyes to see these places that are broken so I can open myself to Your healing and Your truth. In Jesus' name. Amen.

DAY 41

The Underbelly

*"This will result in your being witnesses to them.
But make up your mind not to worry beforehand
how you will defend yourselves. For I will give you
words and wisdom that none of your adversaries
will be able to resist or contradict."*

(LUKE 21:13 – 15)

Thought for the Day: "Criticism may not be agreeable, but it is necessary. It fulfills the same function as pain in the human body. It calls attention to an unhealthy state of things." — WINSTON CHURCHILL

Criticism stinks. That's usually my first thought when someone makes it clear they don't like something I've done or said.

My pride says, "How dare you!"

My heart says, "I want a chance to explain."

My soul says, "Jesus, am I off base?"

My mind says, "Why do I open myself up like this?"

My feelings say, "Ouch."

Sometimes criticism is fair. Maybe I messed up and it would serve me well to reconsider. Other times criticism is nothing but rotten spew. And boy, does it stink. But if I get stuck in the stink, it serves no good purpose.

Might there be another way to look at harsh criticism? To get past the hurt to see if it has an underbelly I should consider?

The other day I Googled the word *underbelly* and stumbled on an article about the armadillo lizard. This fascinating creature has hard and pointy scales that have "Don't mess with me" written all over them. But, like all tough creatures, this lizard has a vulnerable place.

The armadillo lizard's tough exterior wraps around its back but softens at the underbelly. When threatened, the lizard grabs its tail and displays a prickly, intimidating posture to keep other creatures away. At that point, the rest of its body serves only one purpose —to hide and protect its most vulnerable part.

So what does a strange desert creature have to do with criticism?

In an effort to protect my underbelly, I sometimes get all wrapped up in myself and tragically forget the underbelly of my critic—the place they are vulnerable and the things they might be hiding and protecting beneath the harsh words and prickly exterior. This is a place they may never let me see. It's the storage place for their hurts and disappointments. It holds the root cause of their skepticism and the anger that probably has very little to do with me. Remember, "the mouth speaks what the heart is full of" (Matthew 12:34). And from the overflow of their underbelly, they spewed.

If I forget the other person's underbelly, I am tempted to start storing up my own hurt, skepticism, anger, and disappointments. If I remember this underbelly, I have a much greater chance to keep it all in perspective. I can let my reaction be a good example to this other person just as Luke 21:13 – 15 reminds us: "This will result in you being witnesses to them. But make up your mind not to worry beforehand how you will defend yourselves. For I will give you words and wisdom that none of your adversaries will be able to resist or contradict." Yes, I must make up my mind not to worry about defending myself. Then I uncoil. And I see the opportunity to witness.

Dear Lord, thank You for this challenge to think about the other person's underbelly before I react to criticism. I know it's a simple step, but it's so hard to live out. Help me to put this truth into practice and to walk in the wisdom You have already given. In Jesus' name. Amen.

DAY 42

My Creative Best

A heart at peace gives life to the body,
but envy rots the bones.
(PROVERBS 14:30)

Thought for the Day: God has a beautiful plan for me — a creative best I can accomplish with my life.

Empty women, oh, how we come unglued.

Especially when the empty rests in the part of our souls where unmet desires restlessly wait. In that dark corner, desperation churns for what could be but isn't, and what we want but still don't have.

What do we long for? A romantic, attentive mate. A true and trusted friend. A child. Then a child who makes me look good. An attentive parent. A certain talent. Opportunity, things, feelings, recognition, a certain body size, financial freedom, a beautiful house ... the list lengthens.

We long for "it" and the deep satisfaction surely found in getting "it." When others around us get "it," we pretend we are happy for them. We make the good girl in us act happy. Maybe part of us is sincere. Maybe not. But in the quiet of a private moment, the gnawing becomes a splitting plow. Oh, how it digs and cuts and unearths the inside of me.

We get empty when we park our minds on comparison thoughts and wallow in them. Nothing good grows in this place; as James says, "Then, after desire has conceived, it gives birth to sin; and sin, when it is full-grown, gives birth to death" (James 1:15). No jealous thought is ever life-giving. Wallowing in jealous thoughts actually leads to death. Death of contentment. Death of friendships. Death of peace. And certainly death of joy.

Jealousy and envy cut deeper and deeper until we bleed empty. We lose perspective on what we do have and soon focus only on what we don't have. It's at this point that we sit back and say, "Okay, I get all that. I know this is truth. I know jealousy isn't good. It's not like I enjoy it, ask for it to haunt me, or even want it in my life. But it's there. So what's a girl to do? Just having someone say *don't feel jealous* doesn't help me. Having someone point out a fault without offering a solution just makes me feel even more unglued."

Amen to that. And the best solution I know — the only solution I know — is pure truth from God's Word.

The Galatians verses about reaping what you sow are part of a larger passage that offers some revealing teaching. It tells us that when we're struggling with jealousy, we need to carry our own load (Galatians 6:4–5).

> Each one should test their own actions. Then they can take pride in themselves alone, without comparing themselves to someone else, for each one should carry their own load.

What does that mean?

It means we need to focus on reasons to celebrate what we have already been given and what we are doing right.

In my book *Becoming More Than a Good Bible Study Girl*, I shared a truth I challenge myself with when jealousy comes knocking: "I'm not equipped to handle what she has, both good and bad —and what she has is always a package deal of both." In other words, I've been assigned a load I can handle. The good and bad in my load are what I should carry. I'm not designed or assigned to carry someone else's load.

Consider the Galatians verses again from *The Message*:

Make a careful exploration of who you are and the work you have been given, and then sink yourself into that. Don't be impressed with yourself. Don't compare yourself with others. Each of you must take responsibility for doing the creative best you can with your own life.

I like the thought of "doing the creative best with [my] own life." When I wish for someone else's life, I waste the limited life energy I've got to face my own challenges and opportunities. God has a beautiful plan for me—a creative best I can accomplish with my life.

Isn't it just like Satan to want to distract me from this? Satan is a liar who steals, kills, and destroys. He wants to steal my attention, kill my joy, and destroy my creative best by making me want what God has entrusted to someone else. In other words, it is a lie straight from Satan that I'd be happier and more content with someone else's load. I wouldn't. It may feel like I would, but feelings are tricky things.

I can look back on many areas of my life and thank God for His protection in this regard. The boys who never asked me out. The strong-willed tendency in my daughter that eventually turned into a passionate tenacity for missions. The opportunity I never got that keeps me humble. All the things I have and don't have are what make up the unique load I've been assigned.

Ultimately, that's why God tells us to concentrate on carrying our own load and avoid comparing and striving for someone else's load —it's for our protection. I see that now. It gives my brain a better place to go when those I-want-what-she-has thoughts start choking the joy from me. And instead of feeling empty, I feel a sense of possibility. I drop seeds of my own creative design and watch the long limbs of purpose start to form.

Dear Lord, thank You for being such a wise and gracious Father and not giving me everything I ask for. Help me as I try to gain control over jealous thoughts that pop into my head. In Jesus' name. Amen.

DAY·43

If Only We Knew

For we do not have a high priest
who is unable to sympathize with our weaknesses,
but we have one who has been tempted in every way,
just as we are — yet was without sin.
Let us then approach the throne of grace with confidence,
so that we may receive mercy and find grace
to help us in our time of need.

(HEBREWS 4:15 – 16)

Thought for the Day: One drop of the Lord's mercy is better than
an ocean of the world's comfort.

Here is my prayer for you today: *May you catch even the slightest
glimpse of the tender mercy of our Lord Jesus. For one drop of the
Lord's mercy is better than an ocean of the world's comfort.*

The marriage situation that seems impossible.

The finances that never balance.

The hope so deferred it makes your heart sick.

The anxiety over a child bent on a wayward path.

The diet you are sick of.

The broken promises of a friend.

The lack of true friends.

The constant messiness always distracting the peace you want in your home.

The impatience and frustration, anger and disappointment of losing it — again.

If only we knew how deeply Jesus understands and cares for us. If only we could see the wonder of His love. The skies He paints, the flowers He blooms, the world He arranges just for us. The love letters He's written to us throughout the Bible.

These are all mercies from Him.

The world will offer us comfort in the form of escapes. We escape to romance novels, movies, magazines, malls, chocolate, vacations, affirmations from friends. Not that any of these things are bad. They aren't. But they are very temporary. They make us feel good in the moment, but that good never stays. We need more and more. Trying to fill our aching hearts with these things is like trying to fill an ocean with a tablespoon. It's never enough. So we clench our fists and keep trying to find something to comfort us.

If only we knew how to stop clenching our fists so that we could open our hands and catch the drops of His tender mercy. If only we knew how to release the weight of trying to fix it all ourselves. If only we knew to stop in the midst of it all and whisper, "Jesus . . . help me." Just a whispered breath formed in the wholeness of His name carries all the power and mercy and wisdom and grace we need to handle what we face.

If only we knew.

If you find yourself wanting to escape today into one of the world's comforts, first invest some time in asking Jesus to help you, show you, and direct you. Specifically, ask Him to help you see and notice His tender mercies. Then you will see that, indeed, one drop of the Lord's mercy is better than an ocean of the world's comfort.

Jesus, I pray that today I would know how high and how deep is the love You have for me. Help me to catch the tender drops of Your mercy and allow myself to fully embrace Your love. Amen.

When There Isn't a Place for the Wedding Portrait

The LORD is good, a refuge in times of trouble.
He cares for those who trust in him.

(NAHUM 1:7)

Thought for the Day: When there's no way to feel better in the moment, you just have to place your feet on the only solid ground there is — God's truth.

Recently a moving truck pulled up to the front of my friend's house. Sometimes moving signifies something exciting and new. Sometimes it doesn't.

This move signified an end. A few hours into the process of emptying her home, one of the movers carried out her wedding portrait. "You want the photographs in the stairwell to go with us, or are you taking those separately in your vehicle?" he asked.

She turned from unhooking the front porch swing. "I'll be taking those separately," she said, the irony not escaping her. Separately. That was how she'd be living her life now. Separate from the neighborhood where her kids had grown up. Separate from her husband. Separate from the way she thought her life would be.

She took the wedding portrait from the mover and a feeling of confusion washed over her heart and mind. She sat down on the front steps and called me. Through her tears she said, "I don't know what to do with this portrait. What do you do with the things that have no place anymore? We built a life together and now there's no more together. There isn't a place for that in my mind. What am I going to do?"

I knew better than to throw out a quippy little bit of Christianese. I once had someone tell me as I stood over my dying sister's bedside, "You just have to let go and let God." I knew the person meant well. But, honestly, it infuriated me. No, I wouldn't throw out something just to fill the uncomfortable silence. Trite sayings weren't going to help my friend. Well-meaning phrases weren't going to crawl in bed with her tonight and hold her broken heart threatening to beat out of her chest.

That would be like holding out a bottle of Elmer's and suggesting it could fix a life that had come completely unglued.

Maybe you've been there. Whether you were sitting in the midst of tears and confusion or you were the one on the other end of the phone trying desperately to know what to say, I understand. Sometimes we just have to acknowledge that good feelings won't be there for a while. And when there's no way to feel better in the moment, you just have to place your feet on the only solid ground there is — God's truth.

His truth won't shift with feelings.

His truth won't drown in a sea of tears.

His truth won't leave you even when your gut-honest cries don't sound so Christian.

I finally said to my friend, "I'm crying with you. I don't have answers, but I do have prayers. And I'm going to write out conversations I have with God so you'll know He's not being silent right now. He sees you. He hears you. And through His truth He will comfort you."

I pulled out my Bible and poured out the hurt and sadness. "God, show me. Show me the right truths. Use my hand to write out some comfort from your Word for my friend."

Me: Lord, I have to tell You it is a hard thing to watch my friend hurt so much. She begged You to help save her marriage and, honestly, we're confused why it all still fell apart.

The Lord: Do the words of Job 17:11 express the way you are feeling? "My days have passed, my plans are shattered, and so are the desires of my heart."

Me: Yes, Lord, and I'm confused. Lord, don't you see her tears? If seeing her sadness breaks my heart, I know it must break Your heart too. It is hard for me to understand why this all happened.

The Lord: Recall the beauty of trusting the only One who can see what is and what is to come. "The LORD is good, a refuge in times of trouble. He cares for those who trust in him" (Nahum 1:7).

Me: I do trust You, Lord. But for everything to end like this is so hard. It just seems so pointless.

The Lord: Oh, nothing I allow is pointless. Nothing you go through is pointless. Even in the midst of hurt, I will work good.

I will work good for her now and I will work good for her in the future. I still have a grand plan and purpose for her. "Listen to advice and accept instruction, and in the end you will be wise. Many are the plans in a man's heart, but it is the LORD's purpose that prevails" (Proverbs 19:20 – 21).

Me: I just need to know why she has to go through this.

The Lord: You don't have to have answers, Lysa. You just need to trust. " 'For my thoughts are not your thoughts, neither are your ways my ways,' declares the LORD. 'As the heavens are higher than the earth, so are my ways higher than your ways and my thoughts than your thoughts' " (Isaiah 55:8 – 9).

Me: But what about the desires of her heart, Lord?

The Lord: I am the only one who even knows the full scope of those desires, Lysa. I will give her new desires and help her so those desires come to pass. Just encourage her to trust Me and make wise choices. "Trust in the LORD and do good; dwell in the land and enjoy safe pasture. Delight yourself in the LORD and he will give you the desires of your heart" (Psalm 37:3 – 4).

After I wrote all this out, I sent it to my friend. It didn't fix her hurt or answer her questions. It didn't give her a place to put those things that seemed to have no place right now. But it did get her to open up God's Word and start having conversations with Him for herself. And as she moves on, this was a good first step to take.

When she felt like she was drowning in her emotions, God's truth, His Word, was the only thing solid enough to stand on. God's truth will never go away. It will never change.

God, once again I come to You as a child. You are the only One who can ultimately lift me up. I trust You and I pray that through all the ups and downs in life, I will learn to trust You in a very personal way. In Jesus' name. Amen.

DAY 45

Comparisons Stink

*Each of you should use whatever gift
you have received to serve others,
as faithful stewards of God's grace in its various forms.
If anyone speaks, they should do so
as one who speaks the very words of God.
If anyone serves, they should do so
with the strength God provides,
so that in all things God may be praised
through Jesus Christ. To him be the glory
and the power for ever and ever. Amen.*

(1 PETER 4:10 – 11)

Thought for the Day: Only when I get out of the shadow of doubt
can I move into the life-giving reality of who God made *me* to be.

Okay, can I just be brutally honest about something? Comparisons
stink. They do.

Just when I think I've gotten to a good place in some area of my

144

life, along comes someone or something else that's better. And my confidence just shrinks back, takes the hand of doubt, and starts ransacking the peace right out of my heart and mind. Yes, there are Scriptures that can help with this. And yes, God can use it for good in my life. But honest to goodness, it's hard on a girl's heart.

Recently, I was put in a situation where something I feel very vulnerable about was held up to another person's near perfection. I was on a beach vacation with several friends who have dancer's legs. And by dancer, I mean like twenty-year-old, ballerina-perfection legs. I guess you could say I have dancer legs too if you are referring to the dancing hippo from *Madagascar*. I can eat healthy and exercise every bit as much as my ballerina friends, but long, lean legs just aren't in my genetic makeup.

So there I was on the beach. My weakness standing beside their strength. My yuck placed next to their glory. And in the private space of my most inner thoughts, I cried. And even more than that, I found myself feeling defeated and convinced this area won't ever be a strength of mine. I wasn't designed for this to be my strength.

Oh, I can make progress, for sure. And heaven knows, I do work on it. And on my good days, I see how God is using this all for good. But when comparison sneaks in, it can be hard. Worse than hard. It can just quite simply make me forget all the strengths I do have. And when I forget, my hearts shifts. I stop being thankful and instead become consumed by that little thing I don't have. What a dangerous place to be.

When I was struggling recently, I later realized I wasn't prayed up. I had not asked God to help keep my focus on Him. I just found myself wallowing—and wallowing isn't of the Lord. Amen? Amen!

I share this because you need to know—I struggle. Just like you. I'm on a journey of learning. Just like you. And I desperately need

God's truth to bump into my weaknesses every single day. Only then can I get out of the shadow of doubt and into the life-giving reality of who God has made *me* to be. And see it as good. Not perfect. Not even close. But good. And good is good.

God, thank You for teaching me today to find my identity in You and to stop the difficult game of comparison. I know as I focus on who I am in You, jealousy won't be the thing that makes me become unglued. Amen.

DAY 46

The Secret
to Conflict Resolution

Pray also for me, that whenever I open my mouth,
words may be given me so that I will fearlessly
make known the mystery of the gospel.
(EPHESIANS 6:19)

Thought for the Day: Don't let your lips or typing fingertips be the first thing that walks into a conflict.

The secret to healthy conflict resolution isn't taking a you-against-me stance. The secret is realizing it's all of us against Satan—he's the real enemy. But this is hard to do when all we see is that flesh-and-blood person standing there who, quite honestly, is planted squarely on the last good nerve we have left.

This moment may seem like the perfect time to set our Christianity on the shelf. In actuality, though, a moment of conflict handled the right way is hands-down one of the grandest opportunities we have to shame Satan back to hell. A Jesus girl who rises up and unexpectedly gives grace when she surely could have done otherwise reveals the power and the mystery of Christ at work—in her life and in the world.

That's why the apostle Paul ends Ephesians 6 by making a specific statement about words—how he wants to use them and the impact he wants them to have. After explaining that Satan is our real enemy, reminding us to put on our spiritual armor each day, and reiterating the absolute necessity of prayer, Paul says one more thing:

> Pray also for me, that whenever I open my mouth, words may be given me so that I will fearlessly make known the mystery of the gospel. (Ephesians 6:19)

The placement of this verse is crucial and intentional. After we remember who the real enemy is—and that the person who hurt us is *not* our enemy—we must carefully consider the words we speak in response. After all, it's one thing to make the mental shift to acknowledge that the person isn't my enemy, but quite another to speak words that make known the mystery of the gospel. What a choice!

Sometimes when I'm hurt, I want the verse to say, "Most of the time when you open your mouth, make known the gospel. But when someone really hurts your feelings, that day is the exception. Feel free to explode all over her."

Or "Most of the time when you open your mouth, make known the gospel. But when someone else has obvious issues, you should make her aware of those issues and heap back on her what she's heaped on you."

Or "Most of the time when you open your mouth, make known the gospel. But if you're feeling unfairly judged, rally other people around your cause and make this other person look as bad as you can."

But that's not what Ephesians 6:19 says. It says I must make the gospel known *whenever* I open my mouth. Is this easy? Of course not! To have any chance at all, I have to develop a strategy in advance for how I will react in situations like these. In advance means I don't wait until I receive the hurtful comment or the shame-on-you email. In a nonemotional, clearheaded moment, I craft a response template. (In the next devotional, you'll see my example of this. Feel free to copy it or craft your own.) Then on that day when another person decides to get all up in your Kool-Aid with their own raw emotions, you can hold on to your soul integrity.

Dear Lord, please help me be a Jesus girl who rises up and gives grace when I am tempted to do otherwise. I want to reveal Your power at work in my responses. In Jesus' name. Amen.

DAY 47

My Response Template

A gentle answer turns away wrath,
but a harsh word stirs up anger.
(PROVERBS 15:1)

Thought for the Day: Choosing a gentle reply doesn't mean you're weak; it actually means you possess a rare and godly strength.

Whether we're face-to-face with someone or sending a written response to someone, we do need to remember there is a big difference between a *reaction* and a *reply*. Reactions are typically harsh words used to prove how wrong the other person is. No good ever comes from this. A gentle reply, on the other hand, "turns away wrath" (Proverbs 15:1). Choosing a gentle reply doesn't mean you're weak; it actually means you possess a rare and godly strength.

I think I'm going to repeat that last sentence, not so much for you but because, glory be, I need it! *Choosing a gentle reply doesn't mean you're weak; it actually means you possess a rare and godly strength.*

In a heated moment of frustration or anger, I need a preplanned template to keep me from spewing. So here's what I came up with for when I need a written response. Of course this same thought pattern can be tweaked slightly and used for face-to-face interactions as well. Feel free to use this one or come up with a version of your own to use the next time you need a written or verbal response.

1. Begin by honoring the one offended.

This isn't easy. We probably won't feel like the other person deserves honor in that moment. And maybe they don't. Do you remember that shame-on-you email I mentioned earlier in this book? The one where the mom was not happy about her daughter not getting an invitation to my daughter's birthday party and, in no uncertain terms, let me know about it? I certainly didn't feel like honoring my offender's words. So I didn't honor her words. I honored her as a person — a person God loves. I have to remember that giving honor reveals more about my character than the character of the other person.

Here's how I did this:

Dear Sally,

I can tell you are a mother who cares deeply for your child.

I honored her by pointing out a good quality I know to be true about her. Even if you have to think really hard about what good qualities your offender has, most everyone does have redeeming qualities.

2. Keep your response short and full of grace.

The wordier we get, the greater the risk we will slip into defensiveness. If something needs to be clarified, keep it concise and wrapped in grace.

Here are the lines I wrote:

A line to acknowledge the expressed hurt: *I understand how hard it can be when we feel our child has been left out. Like you, I hurt when my child hurts.*

A line to clarify my intentions: *Might I share from my heart what I intended when we invited only the girls from Hope's homeroom class? Hope would have invited many more if she could. But this seemed the fairest way to keep the party manageable.*

A line of gentle honesty about the issue at hand: *This has been a hard year on Hope. You are probably aware of the conflicts Hope and your daughter have had. If you'd like to discuss some possible ways we can better guide both girls in their actions and reactions toward one another, I would welcome that.*

And, if an apology is appropriate: *Please accept my most sincere apology for causing you and your daughter hurt.*

A line asking for grace: *Thank you for extending me grace in this situation.*

3. End by extending compassion.

Chances are this person is hurting for reasons that have nothing to do with this situation. Why not be the rare person who offers love to this hard-to-love person: *With more love and compassion than these words can hold, Lysa*

Of course, if it's not possible to sincerely end your note that way, don't fake it. I know some conflicts can make it impossible to wrap everything with love. So maybe your compassionate close might be a simple *Blessings . . . , Thank you . . . ,* or *With grace.*

Please remember, not every harsh email needs a response. I knew mine did. But ask God to help you know when to deal with it and when to simply delete it.

Also, remember not every face-to-face confrontation needs a verbal response either. But when it does, you can easily translate what I've suggested here for an email into a face-to-face conversation. Just mentally keep this in mind: Honor them. Keep it short and wrapped with grace. Extend compassion. Honor, grace, compassion ... HGC.

Dear Lord, I accept the challenge to hold my tongue in order to honor, give grace, and have compassion for others. Please give me the strength to do this today. Thanks so much. In Jesus' name. Amen.

DAY 48

To-Do List Wisdom

Be gracious in your speech.
The goal is to bring out the best
in others in a conversation,
not put them down, not cut them out.
(COLOSSIANS 4:6 MSG)

Thought for the Day: "When you encounter difficulties and contra-dictions, do not try to break them, but bend them with gentleness and time." — FRANCIS DE SALES

Some of us write out our to-do lists each day. Others of us are more creative (less organized), and we keep our lists floating around in our brains or just fly by the seat of our pants.

Either way, all of us have things we need to get done each day.

Recently my thirteen-year-old daughter, Brooke, tweeted her to-do list.

And, y'all, the preciousness of her list made my heart dance with joy. And it challenged me.

She's a relationship-driven gal. I'm a task-oriented gal. Neither is better. However, I'm challenged when I look at Brooke's list and see that she puts as much intentionality into building her relationships each day as she does into accomplishing her tasks.

Are you ready to see the cutest, sweetest to-do list ever written?

1. Bring project for [social studies] on Ashley's laptop
2. Take allergy meds
3. Tell Mom u love her
4. Text Kenzi to tell her if u are going to school
5. Thank Jesus for being there for u
6. Give Daddy a hug
7. Eat breakfast
8. Take shower (hair looks bad)
9. Tell Ashley she is the best big sister
10. Tell Hope she looks really pretty

My to-do lists don't look like this. They are filled with tasks and errands, which aren't bad, but I do need to get more intentional with relationship building, so maybe adding more relationship-oriented items to my list might help me.

Are you more task-oriented or relationship-oriented? What to-do items do you need to get more intentional about—tasks or relationship building?

Maybe, just maybe, we can use Brooke's sweet to-do list to help formulate our Gentle Reply List.

• How can you honor someone who feels offended today?

• How can you show grace to "your people" today?

- How can you show compassion to that hard-to-love person today?

Yesterday we talked about accepting the challenge to hold our tongues and offer a gentle reply instead of spewing. Today, let's ask the Lord to show us how to love those around us, tempering our responses with honor, grace, and compassion.

Dear Lord, thank You for the people You have placed in my life. Even the ones who are sometimes difficult. I want to honor them by showing grace and compassion today. Help me be intentional with my actions and responses. In Jesus' name. Amen.

DAY 49

You Don't Like Me

And the peace of God, which transcends all understanding,
will guard your hearts and your minds in Christ Jesus.
(PHILIPPIANS 4:7)

Thought for the Day: Toxic thoughts leave no room for truth to flourish. And in the absence of truth, lies reign.

Have you ever had thoughts of insecurity so strangling you thought you might choke? Thoughts like . . .

You are not liked.

Who are you to think you could do that?

Why did you say that? Everyone thinks you're annoying.

Your kids just illustrated every inadequacy you have as a mom.

You are invisible.

If you've never had words like these run rampant through your thoughts, lift your hands up in sheer praise.

For the rest of us, let's go there today. Because, honestly, we unglued girls need to go there. To the inner places of secret thoughts and harsh self-condemnations. If there were one gift I wish I could give every woman on the planet, it would be the ability to silence the destructive words we allow to fall hard on our souls. Toxic thoughts leave no room for truth to flourish. And in the absence of truth, lies reign.

The other day I was discussing something with my husband, and I said, "I know you think I'm being annoying and overly protective about this but . . ."

Art stopped me and said, "How do you know that's what I'm thinking? Please don't hold me liable for saying things that are really only thoughts in your mind."

Sheer brilliance.

He's so right. *He* hadn't said those things. I was assuming he was thinking them and operating as if those toxic thoughts were reality.

I think we girls do this way too often. People aren't thinking about us and assessing us nearly as much as we think they are. Honestly, they don't have time. Because they are probably spending too much time thinking about and assessing themselves. Do you see the crazy in all this?

I do.

That's why we've got to hold our thoughts to a higher standard. How dare they be allowed to simply parade about as if they are true and manipulate us into feeling insecure, inadequate, and misunderstood! Oh, how much trouble we invite into our lives when our thoughts are based on assumptions.

So here are three questions we'd do well to ask ourselves when thoughts are dragging us down.

1. Did someone actually say this or am I making assumptions about what they're thinking?

If they actually said it, then I need to deal with it. If I'm assuming it, that's unfair to them and damaging to me. Philippians 4:6 invites me to choose prayer over worry in every situation. Instead of allowing my thoughts to overtake me, whether in assumptions or despair, I can ask God to shine His truth into my situation. "Do not be anxious about anything, but in everything by prayer and supplication with thanksgiving let your requests be made known to God" (NASB).

2. Am I actively immersing myself in truth?

The more I read God's truths and let truth fill my mind, the less time I'll spend contemplating untruths. Philippians 4:7 holds a promise for me when I turn to God and allow His truth to fill me: my heart is protected by peace. "And the peace of God, which surpasses all comprehension, will guard your hearts and your minds in Christ Jesus" (NASB).

3. Are there situations or relationships that feed my insecurities?

If so, maybe I need to take a break from these for a season. "Finally, brothers and sisters, whatever is true, whatever is noble, whatever is right, whatever is pure, whatever is lovely, whatever is admirable — if anything is excellent or praiseworthy — think about such things" (Philippians 4:8).

Good gracious, I know this is tough stuff. I know these issues can be more complicated than three simple questions. But it's a good place to start holding our thoughts accountable.

After all, how a woman thinks is often how she lives.

I think we need to read that one again, don't you? *How a woman thinks is often how she lives.* May we think on and live out truth — and only truth — today.

Dear Lord, fix my heart and mind on You today so that I will experience Your peace. Help me recognize and control unhealthy thoughts. In Jesus' name. Amen.

DAY 50

I Don't Think You're Wacky

You will always harvest what you plant.
(GALATIANS 6:7 NLT)

Thought for the Day: Friendships are like plowed open fields ready for growth. What we plant is what will grow.

Inside chatter is such a crazy thing. Last week, I had a funny conversation with a friend. We were having coffee when she admitted she'd been having inside chatter about something she'd said to me on the phone the night before. She went to bed kicking herself for saying something she felt was dumb and was certain I thought she was a bit wacky.

I absolutely didn't go to bed thinking she was the least bit wacky. Quite the opposite. I went to bed thinking she is one of the cutest, nicest people I know. So I quieted her inside chatter by planting seeds of reassurance.

Friendships are like plowed open fields ready for growth. What we plant is what will grow. If we plant seeds of reassurance, blessing, and love, we reap a great harvest of security. Of course, if we plant seeds of backbiting, questioning, and doubt, we reap a great harvest of insecurity.

Indeed, today is a great day to call a friend and say, "You don't have to worry about me having negative thoughts about you. If I need to talk to you about something, I will. Otherwise, you can rest assured I am always believing the best about you. I love you. That's all I'm thinking. Period."

I've discovered that the more love and joy I plant in others, the more love and joy I experience in my own life. But I only have that flourishing joy when I focus on God's truth in my life. Here is a passage that would make a lovely lead song for the soundtrack of our lives as we seek to keep from becoming unglued and help our friends do the same:

> Our mouths were filled with laughter, our tongues with songs of joy. Then it was said among the nations, "The LORD has done great things for them." The LORD has done great things for us, and we are filled with joy. (Psalm 126:2–3)

Wouldn't this be a wonderful truth to live out in our lives and spread to the lives of our friends? I want to have this kind of love and joy; therefore I need to invest in giving to others this kind of love and joy. After all, it's what we give to others that often spreads back into our life. Indeed, what we plant is what we'll harvest.

Dear Lord, today I am choosing to plant joy and love and encouragement in my friendships. Please help me to love my friends well today. In Jesus' name. Amen.

DAY 51

The Friendship Challenge

Perfume and incense bring joy to the heart,
and the pleasantness of a friend springs
from their heartfelt advice.
(PROVERBS 27:9)

Thought for the Day: Establishing real intimacy with a friend requires pushing past the resistance, the fear, and our unglued reactions.

What makes a woman tender also reveals her vulnerabilities.

What makes a woman transparent also exposes her wounds.

What makes a woman authentic also uncovers her insecurities.

And there isn't a woman alive who likes being revealed, exposed, and uncovered. But to establish real intimacy with a friend requires pushing past this resistance, past the fear, and past our unglued reactions. To be known is to risk being hurt.

Friendship is risky. But friendship can be beautiful.

I want you to think about a friend in whom you can make an

investment this week. I challenge you not to think of the friend with whom you feel most comfortable. Rather, think of the friend who might benefit from seeing a little more of your tenderness, transparency, and authenticity.

There is someone in your sphere of influence who feels desperate to know that someone else understands.

Might you take three days and give her three friendship investments?

Day 1: Have a conversation with her in which you honestly admit one of your vulnerabilities or insecurities. Chances are, she'll reveal something of herself to you as well. Then commit, really commit, to praying for her.

Maybe wear your watch on the opposite wrist. Every time you're distracted by this out-of-sorts placement, use it as a prompt to pray for your friend. Think of the burden she's been carrying lately and carry it in your prayers this day.

Day 2: Buy this friend a gift—just because. It doesn't have to cost much, but make an investment of time to think of something that would really be delightful to her.

Day 3: Write your friend a note to attach to the gift. In the note, tell her at least three things you admire about her and acknowledge some way she's made a difference in your life. Then deliver this little just-because gift and note to your friend. This friend who sometimes feels a little vulnerable. Wounded. Exposed in some way.

Your honesty and thoughtfulness will be such a sweet investment —for her, for you, for your friendship.

Being vulnerable in a friendship is a great way to pave the road to the kind of honesty that keeps our relationships healthy.

Are you up for taking the friendship challenge?

Dear Lord, thank You for the friends you have given me and thank You for this sweet reminder today. Help me to expose those vulnerable, hard-to-reach places with my friend. I want to show Your love through this challenge. In Jesus' name. Amen.

DAY 52

The Scribbled Truth
That Changed My Life

The LORD your God is with you, the Mighty Warrior who saves.
He will take great delight in you; in his love he will no longer
rebuke you, but will rejoice over you with singing.

(ZEPHANIAH 3:17)

Thought for the Day: Never doubt the power of a simple note. Especially when it contains God's Word that will go forth and will accomplish things human reasoning can't.

When my baby sister died tragically and unexpectedly, my entire world flipped upside down. That season of my life was very dark. What I knew to be true suddenly became questionable.

Is God good? If so, why this? And if I never find out why, how can I ever trust God again?

Hard questions. Honest questions. Questions that haunted me. Until.

One day I got a note from a friend. A young woman I not so affectionately called my "Bible friend." She honestly got on my nerves with all her Bible verse quoting. I wasn't on good terms with God at that point in my life. I didn't want to believe God even existed. And I certainly wasn't reading the Bible.

I made all of this plainly clear to my Bible friend. But in her sweet and kind way, she kept slipping me notes gently woven through, with verses of truth. And then one day, one of those verses cracked the dam of my soul.

"For I know the plans I have for you," declares the LORD, "plans to prosper you and not to harm you, plans to give you hope and a future." (Jeremiah 29:11)

Truth slipped in and split open my hard-hearted views of life just enough for God to make Himself known to me.

Personally. Intimately. Relentlessly.

I held that simple note with one Bible verse scribbled on the front as tears of honest need streamed down my cheeks. My stiff knees bent. And a whispered "Yes, God," changed the course of my life.

I will never doubt the power of a simple note again. Especially when it contains God's Word that will go forth and accomplish things human reasoning can't. I love that about God's Word.

If there is a note you need to send to someone today, here are some of my favorite verses of truth from God's Word you might include (today's key verse is another):

This is the confidence we have in approaching God: that if we ask anything according to his will, he hears us. (1 John 5:14)

I sought the LORD, and he answered me; he delivered me from all my fears. (Psalm 34:4)

Therefore, since we are receiving a kingdom that cannot be shaken, let us be thankful, and so worship God acceptably with reverence and awe. (Hebrews 12:28)

Let us hold unswervingly to the hope we profess, for he who promised is faithful. (Hebrews 10:23)

May the Lord direct your hearts into God's love and Christ's perseverance. (2 Thessalonians 3:5)

The Sovereign LORD is my strength; he makes my feet like the feet of a deer, he enables me to tread on the heights. (Habakkuk 3:19)

The LORD is good, a refuge in times of trouble. He cares for those who trust in him. (Nahum 1:7)

And what does the LORD require of you? To act justly and to love mercy and to walk humbly with your God. (Micah 6:8)

Finally, brothers and sisters, whatever is true, whatever is noble, whatever is right, whatever is pure, whatever is lovely, whatever is admirable — if anything is excellent or praiseworthy — think about such things. (Philippians 4:8)

That one note from my Bible friend took my unglued heart and put the most important missing piece into place ... Jesus. Never underestimate the power of scribbling a few truths to a friend. It just might change her life.

Dear Lord, Your Word is a precious lamp to my feet. Help me hold it high to shine truth on the questions along my path. Thanks for Your hope. In Jesus' name. Amen.

DAY 53

Pizza Man Grace

Be angry, and yet do not sin;
do not let the sun go down on your anger,
and do not give the devil an opportunity.
(EPHESIANS 4:26 – 27 NASB)

Thought for the Day:
Accumulated Aggravations = Accumulated Impact

The pizza guy held a delivery bag too small for the requested four larges. I opened the door and smiled. "Four large pizzas, right?"

The look on his face told me the many teens in my backyard were about to be really disappointed. He said, "Ummm, well, actually there's only two. Let me check your ticket ... oh yeah, you're supposed to have four. Give me twenty minutes, and I'll be back with the other two."

I took the two he had and said, "Oh, no problem. The kids can start on these and then have round two when you get back."

As I walked into the kitchen, Art gave me a funny look. "I thought you ordered four pizzas."

"Yeah, the delivery guy forgot two of them but will be back in a few minutes. No big deal," I quipped with a shoulder shrug.

Art tilted his head. "You didn't even ask for a discount or coupons or anything?"

"Oh honey, I felt bad for the guy. It's not a big deal to ask the kids to wait for a few minutes." I smiled.

Thinking of the way I'd reacted during a little "growth opportunity" we'd had earlier, Art said, "Wow. I'd like to get that kind of grace."

Ouch. The point was well made. I'd gotten very aggravated with something Art had done and let him know it. Why is it I'm so quick to give a gentle answer to a stranger but spew on those I love the most?

I think it's because of accumulated impact.

This was the only time I'd ever seen the pizza guy. My emotions toward him were completely neutral. When he made a mistake, I was able to just let it go.

But I have a history with Art. We do lots of life together. If I let little aggravations collect, my emotions ratchet up, creating more and more tension. Then when something happens, I find it much harder to brush it off. Accumulated aggravations … accumulated impact.

Therefore, it's crucial I don't collect aggravations. I've heard the verse many times: "Do not let the sun go down on your anger" (Ephesians 4:26 NASB). I know it. But honestly, sometimes I ignore it. I go to bed mad anyhow. I collect the aggravations because I'm too tired to talk. Or I don't want to deal with it. Or I try to convince myself it's not a big deal to go to bed mad.

Yet if I keep reading one more verse — Ephesians 4:27 — I understand why I should deal with little aggravations when they are still little. They might not stay little long. Why? Because verse 27 finishes with a strong warning: "Do not give the devil an opportunity."

Yikes.

The devil is just waiting for me to give him an opportunity. I picture him looking at me getting mad over the stupidest things, and hissing, "Go to bed mad … go to bed mad … oh yes, go to bed mad and give me an opportunity." That thought sends shivers down my spine.

As well it should.

I love my man. I get aggravated with my man. But I love him. So I certainly don't want to open the door of opportunity for the devil to turn small aggravations into big ones.

So I put down the pizza and kissed my man's cheek. "I love you, and I'm sorry I didn't give you that kind of grace."

To which he replied back with a big smile, "I still think we should have asked for a discount or coupons."

Like I said, I love this man!

Dear Lord, I really want to follow Your example and live a life full of grace. Help me show grace to those closest to me. I don't want to give the devil any opportunities in my marriage, in my relationships with my children, or in my friendships. In Jesus' name. Amen.

DAY 54

The Best Worst Thing

*And we know that in all things God works
for the good of those who love him.*
(ROMANS 8:28)

Thought for the Day: God can take our worst and add His best.
We just have to make the choice to stay with Him and keep following
Him through it all.

I failed at being a wedding planner. No one wants a planner who
gets so undone by the neurotic mother of the bride that she throws
up in the parking lot right beside the guest sidewalk. Really, nothing
says, "Welcome to my wedding," quite like that.

I failed at being a kitchen gadget saleswoman. No one wants to
see the tip of a thumb sliced off into the veggie pizza at the exact
moment I was promising how safe this gadget is. Awesome.

I failed at being a cafeteria lady at a private school. My assistant
decided her arms were so dry she needed to coat herself with our
spray butter. When we took the trash out later that day, we both got

attacked by bees and forgot about the pizza in the oven. Kids don't take kindly to burnt pizza.

I failed at being a receptionist. It's never a good idea to just succumb to those sleepy afternoon feelings and lay your head down on the desk. Bosses don't like workers who snore. Even if they are pregnant.

Yes, I failed at a lot during those years when I was trying to figure out what to do with my life. At the time, each of these things felt like the worst thing that could have happened. Now I think they were the *best worst things*.

Had I been successful at these things, I never would have discovered the joy of being in the ministry I'm in now. I see this same theme woven throughout many stories in the Bible.

Jesus is getting into a boat with His disciples. "Without warning, a furious storm came up on the lake, so that the waves swept over the boat" (Matthew 8:23 – 24). Worst thing. But then Jesus gets up and rebukes the winds and waves, and things turn completely calm. The disciples are amazed. *Best worst thing.*

The apostles are being arrested and thrown in jail (Acts 5:12). Worst thing. But then an angel of the Lord opens the doors of the jail and brings them out. Later, they are so full of confidence they boldly proclaim, "We must obey God rather than human beings!" (Acts 5:29). *Best worst thing.*

Jesus is crucified and dies on a cross. Worst thing. But then on the third day he rises from the grave, making a way for us to be forgiven from our sins. *Best worst thing.*

I don't understand why we have to go through cruddy stuff. And I certainly know there are far worse things to go through than a few job changes.

We live in a broken world full of broken people. But isn't it comforting to know God is never broken? He isn't ever caught off guard, taken by surprise, or shocked by what happens next.

He can take our worst and add His best. We just have to make the choice to stay with Him and keep following Him through it all.

Even a neurotic mother of the bride who makes a wedding planner's stomach work in reverse can become a *best worst thing*.

Dear Lord, I can't begin to say how grateful I am that You turn all things for good. All things. Give me faith to believe and see. Thanks so much. In Jesus' name. Amen.

DAY 55

Advice to Unglued Wives: Stop Praying

Love is patient, love is kind. It does not envy,
it does not boast, it is not proud. It does not dishonor others,
it is not self-seeking, it is not easily angered,
it keeps no record of wrongs. Love does not delight
in evil but rejoices with the truth. It always protects,
always trusts, always hopes, always perseveres.

(1 CORINTHIANS 13:4 – 7)

Thought for the Day: God isn't looking for me to be a "fix-him" wife. God is looking for me to be a "love-him" wife.

Irritated. Frustrated. Hurt.

Those were the words bumping around in my mind as I grabbed my Bible and sat down for some sort of quiet time. I felt like such a fake, mindlessly scanning these holy words on thin pages. My heart wasn't connecting. My mind wasn't tuned in. All I could think about was the argument I'd had with my husband.

Why couldn't he see my point? Why didn't he understand? Why was he being so stubborn?

I closed my Bible and decided a much more productive thing to do with this situation was to pray. That's what godly women do. And oh, how spiritually sound I felt listing all the many things the Lord could do to fix my man — all that was wrong with him. Sounds spiritual. However, it was anything but.

Suddenly, in the middle of my prayer, I could sense God saying, "Stop!"

Stop? Stop praying? Well, that certainly couldn't be from the Lord . . . so I kept going.

But the word *stop* was pulsing through my mind with each beat of my heart. And deep in my heart, I started to sense why.

God wasn't looking for me to be a "fix-him" wife.

God was looking for me to be a "love-him" wife.

I needed to stop praying. At least, I needed to stop praying the way I had been. Yes, there were things my husband needed to work on. But nothing good was happening when all I did was complain about him.

I needed to be a wife daring enough to ask God to reveal to me how to love my husband. And I needed to ask God where I was going wrong, where I was being selfish, where I needed to work.

When I shifted my focus to letting God change me, that's when I started to see real progress.

In this season of struggling through all of this, God taught me powerful lessons through three questions:

1. Is this an irritation or an issue?

There is a big difference between an irritation and an issue. Identifying the difference helps me pick my battles. If this is just an irritation, maybe I need to practice being more flexible, patient, or willing to extend grace.

2. Am I praying about *my husband* or for *my husband*?

If I do sense something that needs to change, I need to pray for my husband, not about him. Praying about him is just ranting. Praying for him means digging into God's Word and praying Scriptures specific to his struggles. That's powerful! When we pray the *Word* of God, we pray the *will* of God.

3. Where is my focus?

I'll never be able to control how another person acts and reacts, but I certainly can control how I act and react. My focus shouldn't be on *having* the right partner. My focus should be on *being* the right partner.

Slowly, as I shifted my heart in these areas, I saw great progress in our marriage. Do I still get irritated, frustrated, and hurt? Of course. But when I stopped trying to fix my husband, I was freed up to just love him. And that's a much more fun and realistic job for me.

Dear Lord, help me to stop focusing on being a "fix-him" wife and instead focus on being a "love-him" wife. In Jesus' name. Amen.

DAY 56

Pinches and Grace

Let us then approach God's throne
of grace with confidence,
so that we may receive mercy and find grace
to help us in our time of need.

(HEBREWS 4:16)

Thought for the Day:
Today is a beautiful time for grace.

I wanted to pinch the two girls sitting on the front row of our church service. Pinch them, I tell you. But they were five rows ahead of me, and my arm couldn't quite reach. Since I couldn't physically get their attention, I prepared my "look." You know, the one that says a thousand corrective statements with just a cross expression and a raised eyebrow? Yes, that one.

The minute one of them stole a glance in my direction, they were gonna know exactly how I felt about their wiggling and obvious lack of attention during the service. Oh, and might I mention, these two girls belonged to me. Well, at least one of them did. The other was my daughter's friend, who sometimes goes to church with us.

I don't think anyone else really noticed them. They weren't being disruptive to other people. But they weren't acting the way I wanted them to. I wanted them sitting up straight, drinking in the message, and taking pages of notes. Thank you very much.

Suddenly, an annoying little thought started to tug at the corners of my mind. *You want your children to act perfectly because it makes you look good. Let that go. They don't need to be sitting up straight, furiously taking notes, to hear God's message. This is a beautiful time for grace. And when you give grace ... you won't come unglued.*

Ouch.

I don't much like the Holy Spirit speaking to me the kind of truth that hurts. I was in the mood to pinch somebody. Two somebodies. Give grace? Now? It wasn't what I wanted, but it was exactly what I needed to do in that moment.

Soon my daughter's friend peered back to look at me. Despite my feelings, I made the choice to smile, wink, and give her a little wave. Then this wiggly, usually not-very-affectionate middle schooler got out of her seat, walked back the aisle five rows, threw her arms around me, and gave me a hug that preached a thousand sermons right then and there.

Indeed, grace was exactly what was needed in that moment.

And that's what makes this parenting thing so stinkin' hard. There are really no textbook answers. Only God can prepare me with the wisdom and discernment necessary for each and every potentially unglued parenting moment.

It's such a moment-by-moment balancing act of loving, shepherding, disciplining, extending grace, molding, modeling, loving some more, and maybe having to give a few pinches along the way too.

God, I pray that today You would give me the strength to stay close to You to experience Your grace and give Your grace. Open my eyes to the challenging situations around me that need a dusting of Your grace. Amen.

DAY 57

Sometimes We Just Have to Get Quiet

And the God of all grace, who called you to his eternal glory
in Christ, after you have suffered a little while,
will himself restore you and make you strong, firm and steadfast.
To him be the power for ever and ever. Amen.

(1 PETER 5:10 – 11)

Thought for the Day: I want to be a passionate woman reined in by God's grace — not an exploder who shames herself.

Remember that our goal, whether we are exploding and shaming ourselves or exploding and blaming others, is imperfect progress. When I've had an explosion, I feel a lot more *imperfect* than I do *progress*. We're dealing with emotions and relationships — both of which are like nailing Jell-O to the wall. It's a complicated, messy, and unpredictable process, for sure. Sometimes a girl can get worn out, wonder if she's ever going to really stop exploding, and feel like giving up.

But before I give up, I've learned to hush up. This often means hitting a pause button on whatever situation is making me feel like exploding. Ideally, this would mean getting away by myself in the quiet of my home. Sometimes this means excusing myself to the restroom. Bathroom stalls can make great prayer closets (smile). The point is that the only way I can see what God is doing and attend to what He reveals is to get quiet with Him.

Here are five beautiful things I've discovered in the quiet with God—straight from Scripture in 1 Peter 5:6–10. They are balm for the raw edges of a soul on the precipice of exploding.

1. In the quiet, we feel safe enough to humble ourselves.

The last thing I want to do in the heat of an emotional mess is to be humble. I want to be loud and proud and to prove my point. But I've learned the hard way that I have to step out of the battle and humbly ask God to speak truth to my heart in order for things to start making sense. Never have I had a relationship issue in which I didn't contribute at least something to the problem. Usually, I can only see this something in the quiet. The quiet is what enables us to "humble [ourselves], therefore, under God's mighty hand" (1 Peter 5:6).

2. In the quiet, God lifts us up to a more rational place.

When we are in the heat of a tangled mess, crazy emotions drag us down into a pit of hopelessness. The only way out of the pit is to make the choice to stop digging deeper and turn to God for a solution, so "that [God] may lift you up in due time" (1 Peter 5:6).

3. In the quiet, anxiety gives way to progress.

We can pour out our anxious hearts to Jesus, who loves us right where we are, just as we are. Because His love comes without unfair human judgment, we soften and feel safe enough to humbly admit we need Jesus to work on us. Trying to fix another person only adds to my anxiety. Letting Jesus work on me is where real progress happens. I claim the promise of 1 Peter 5:7: "Cast all your anxiety on him because he cares for you."

4. In the quiet, we acknowledge that our real enemy isn't the other person.

This person with whom we're in conflict may seem like the enemy and they might even look like the enemy. But the truth is, they aren't the real culprit. The real culprit is Satan, who is exerting influence on both me and the person offending me. I don't always realize this in the heat of the moment, but in the quiet, I can remind myself of the truth and choose a strategy for responding with self-control. That's the wisdom of Scripture, which says, "Be self-controlled and alert. Your enemy the devil prowls around like a roaring lion looking for someone to devour. Resist him, standing firm in the faith" (1 Peter 5:8–9).

5. In the quiet, I can rest assured God will use this conflict for good—no matter how it turns out.

If I make the effort to handle this conflict well, I can be freed from the pressure to make everything turn out rosy. Sometimes relationships grow stronger through conflict; other times relationships end. Because I can't control the other person, I must keep focusing on the good God is working out in me through this and leave the outcome with Him. God's Word promises that "the God of all grace, who called you to his eternal glory in Christ, after you have suffered a little while, will himself restore you and make you strong, firm and steadfast" (1 Peter 5:10).

Maybe you can add to this list as you discover your own benefits in getting quiet when all you really want to do is explode.

Imperfect progress.

Can you sense you're making your way toward this goal?

Oh God, help me. I want to be a passionate woman reined in by You and Your grace. I want to learn to hold my tongue and keep the Holy Spirit's power working in me. Help these truths sink in and become part of who I am and how I live. In Your sweet name. Amen.

DAY 58

Space to Exhale

"If you keep your feet from breaking the Sabbath
and from doing as you please on my holy day,
if you call the Sabbath a delight and the LORD's holy day
honorable, and if you honor it by not going your own way
and not doing as you please or speaking idle words,
then you will find your joy in the LORD."

(ISAIAH 58:13–14)

Thought for the Day:
The Sabbath isn't merely a time to be observed;
it's a time to be preserved.

It's good to be reminded that the reality of true Sabbath is in Christ. In Him we see a picture of grace. And in grace we can be vulnerable enough to be completely honest *with* ourselves *about* ourselves.

Completely honest.

There are honest, personal reasons we need to observe the Sabbath that will be unique for each person. There are private conversations we need to have with God. We all need to hit pause, sit with God, and ask Him to reveal some things to us.

And when I consider Isaiah 58:13–14, something profound occurs to me—it's not just a day for me to give to God. It's a day that God has something He wants to give me if only I'll slow down enough to receive it. "If you keep your feet from breaking the Sabbath and from doing as you please on my holy day, if you call the Sabbath a delight and the LORD's holy day honorable, and if you honor it by not going your own way and not doing as you please or speaking idle words, then you will find your joy in the LORD." The Sabbath isn't merely a time to be observed; it's a time to be preserved. It's a time to rediscover our joy in the Lord. Yes! I need this. I want to be a preserver of this day—one who is determined to set aside this day of personal preservation and rediscovered joy.

The observer remembers to rest.

The preserver rests to remember—to remember that it's all about God.

The observer remembers to rest and pause on the Sabbath day in order to follow a rule. The preserver does more than follow a rule. She follows God's desire and embraces God's purpose in the rest. She spends one day a week letting the fresh wind of God's rest blow through her, cleaning out all she's been taking in during the week with a purifying soul exhale.

It's all about pausing and connecting with God without the distracting chaos of our everyday routines. For one day a week, we step out of the fray and let God direct our day according to His rhythm, not ours. God's rhythm preserves the best in us, reveals the places we're getting off track, and prevents us from being filled with unnecessary clutter. Once we see clutter—the places where we're going our own way, the areas where we're more self-pleasing than God-pleasing, the idle words that need to be reined in—we can deal with the clutter.

The Sabbath makes this possible.

Taking this one day for rest gives my soul the freedom it so desperately needs. Freedom to breathe. Space to breathe. Inhaling and exhaling in a gentle rhythm set by God. This is what my son Mark is really good at. It's not just that his brain can rest and think no thoughts. He really knows how to embrace space for his soul to breathe.

And you know what? I've never seen Mark come unglued. Never. This is partly because he has a beautiful temperament. But it is also because he knows what it means to find his joy in Christ. In grace. In Sabbath. I once asked Mark, "How is it you don't get angry when your brother does something to annoy you?"

"Simple," he replied. "If he's getting on my nerves, I just tell him not to do that. And if he keeps doing it, I walk away." He inhales the issue and then exhales it with grace.

Alrighty then. No need to get all angry and complicated and overanalyzing. Just an honest assessment from a soul who is rested enough to stay calm. Joy, rest, grace. Yes, I want more of this Sabbath.

Dear Lord, space to breathe, this is what I need today. Thank You for showing me how important it is to create this space. In Jesus' name. Amen.

Soul Rest

"Come to Me, all who are weary and heavy-laden,
and I will give you rest. Take My yoke upon you
and learn from Me, for I am gentle and humble in heart,
and you will find rest for your souls.
For My yoke is easy and My burden is light."
(MATTHEW 11:28–30 NASB)

Thought for the Day:
Where there is a lack of Sabbath rest,
there is an abundance of stress.

I was in the kitchen the other day with my teenage son. He was stirring a pot of rice and I was sorting through the day's mail. It was a rare, quiet moment in my house when all the other kids were gone, so I wanted to make the most of an opportunity to connect with him.

"Mark, what are you thinking about?"

"Nothing," he replied. And I knew from the gentle way the word slowly tumbled out, it wasn't a brush-off. But how in heavens could he be thinking about nothing? I had to know.

"So when you say nothing, do you really mean nothing? Or do you mean you are thinking about something you don't want to tell me about?"

"No," he said. "I mean I'm really not thinking about anything right now."

"How is that possible?" I asked. "Like, you don't have one thing you are worried about or a conversation you're rehashing or a bunch of lists you are mentally reviewing in your mind?"

He tilted his head and looked at me like I was one giant unplucked eyebrow. "Ummm . . . nope."

Amazing. Truly amazing. And challenging. I think I need to be a little more like Mark when it comes to emotional white space. Although he may be wired with the ability to easily enter into a place of mental rest, God is calling me to incorporate more times of rest into my life. I desperately need them.

Rest sounds so good, but it is difficult for a girl like me. Even when my physical body is at rest, my mind rarely is. Can you relate?

It's tough. And yet the Bible makes it very clear that we are to make time for rest. More than just physical rest, we need to take a spiritual and emotional rest from going our own way — literally. Once a week, we are to hit the pause button on life and guard a day of rest for our souls. Guard it fiercely and intentionally — even if the demands on our schedules beg us not to.

This is hard for me. I'm not good at pausing and letting my soul enter into Sabbath rest. I haven't come close to mastering this and I am far from being a Sabbath heroine. But I am a messenger who has been trying to make some imperfect progress in this area. Because I know where there is a lack of Sabbath rest, there is an abundance of stress. And where there is an abundance of stress, there is great potential for me to eventually come unglued.

Father, finding rest in my busy life often seems impossible. But I am a woman desperate to find this place of rest. Please open my heart to find this place where You so long to renew my life each week. Amen.

DAY 60

No More Unglued Mama Mornings

You were taught, with regard to your former way of life,
to put off your old self, which is being corrupted
by its deceitful desires; to be made new in the attitude
of your minds; and to put on the new self,
created to be like God in true righteousness and holiness.
(EPHESIANS 4:22–24)

Thought for the Day: I want to be an uncommon calm in the midst of chaos and an example of peace for my kids in a world of pressure.

Well, have you made imperfect progress through this journey? Are you ready to put all that we've learned to the test? Me too. So I'm starting with one of the situations in which I most often find myself coming unglued: school mornings. I'm making a bold commitment: no more unglued mama mornings. In other words, I want our mornings to go better this year with less frustration, yelling, and chaos.

I started thinking about this recently when we had a string of really hard mornings.

One day, as I pulled up to the front of the school, the atmosphere inside the car was thick with tension. Not wanting the last words spoken to my middle-school daughter to be harsh, I tried to change the course of our conversation before she headed into her day. "Listen, I love you. I'm sorry we had a rough morning."

"We always have rough mornings," she shot back before getting out of the car and slamming the door.

Well, nothing makes a mom feel more successful than a little dialogue like that.

As I rubbed the stabbing feeling in my chest, I thought to myself, *Something has got to change. Each day I promise myself I won't yell at the kids in the morning and yet every day I do. I don't want to. But each morning something happens that triggers me to just lose it.*

Ever been there?

It's not like we wake up in the mood to get frustrated with our people, right? I mean, honestly, I usually wake up in a pretty good mood. But then the stress of getting everyone ready and to school on time makes the crazy creep in. This one can't find her shoes. That one needs a report printed, and we have no ink in the printer. The dog just had an accident on the new rug because no one listened to my instructions to let her out. The bread for sandwiches is still sitting on the grocery store shelf because I forgot to buy it yesterday. And to top it all off, I have no cash to give the kids so they can buy their lunch at school.

The whining. The complaining. The feeling that I just can't ever get it all together. It all just escalates and sends me over the edge.

Well, I want mornings from now on to be different. I want to be like our key verse today: "made new in the attitude of my mind."

The Greek word for "made new" is *kaino*, which has as one of its definitions "uncommon." Yes, that's what I want. I want to be an uncommon calm in the midst of chaos and an example of peace for my kids in a world of pressure. If that's going to happen, then I need a strategy. Here's what I've come up with:

1. Tell the world to wait.

When I wake up, my mind is like a dry sponge. What I soak up first will saturate me most deeply. If I don't want to be consumed with the stresses of my day, I must soak up what will renew my mind instead: God's Word. Even if it's only for five minutes, I've got to put the world on hold until I've checked in with God.

2. Remember I'm managing blessings.

If I want my attitude to be made new, I must keep things in perspective. While my frustrations seem big, lost shoes, no ink in the printer, and less-than-perfectly-packed lunches aren't big problems. They are small aggravations that come with managing blessings. I'm managing blessings. Oh God, help me see that.

3. Let my kids take responsibility for their own actions or inactions.

My kids' irresponsibility will not become my emergency. I need to communicate my expectations to the kids so they know they are going to have to own the consequences of their choices. For example, if they wait until the last minute to print their report and the printer has no ink, then they can't print their report. They'll either have to figure out how to print it at school or turn it in late. Either way, I can't take responsibility for this situation or let it throw me into frantic, fix-it mode. I let the consequences of their choices scream so I don't have to.

All of this is going to take some intentionality, and no doubt I won't do it all perfectly. But I'm excited about trying. I'm excited to "put on my new self, created to be like God in true righteousness and holiness." Which is a fancy way of saying I'm excited to have fewer unglued mama mornings and a lot more peace this year.

What's an area of your life in which you want to have fewer unglued moments? Determine to take all we've learned during this sixty-day journey and start applying it there. Make some imperfect progress. And be amazed as you start to make wise choices in the midst of situations where before you would have come unglued.

Dear Lord, thank You for the grace You give me every day. I don't want to live in the same pattern of coming unglued anymore. Lord, help me put these principles into practice. I know these changes won't be easy and I know I can only make them with Your help. Please help me. In Jesus' name. Amen.

NOTE: Struggles with raw emotions may occasionally reach serious levels. If you or a loved one think you might be displaying unhealthy, even harmful, expressions of anger or depression, please seek out a professional counselor.

APPENDIX

Determine
Your Reaction Type

In Chapters 4–6 of the *Unglued* book we discussed the four different reaction types:

- Exploder that Blames Others
- Exploder that Shames Herself
- Stuffer that Builds Barriers
- Stuffer that Collects Retaliation Rocks

To help you determine your reaction type, you can take the more extensive assessment at *www.Ungluedbook.com*. But first, complete the simple inventory (pages 198–201) to get an initial idea of your reaction type.

When you complete this inventory, concentrate on one relationship at a time. As we discussed in the chapters, our reactions change with different relationships.

1. Think of one person in your life: your mother, spouse, child, boss, etc.

2. When you have a conflict with this person, are you more likely to want to process your frustration outwardly? Or are you more likely to stew about it internally?

   • If you process by stewing or by needing to get by yourself to think before deciding to address it or not, you are more than likely an internal processer with this person and fall into the top half of the diagram below.

   • If you process by talking or yelling about it, you are more than likely an external processer with this person and fall into the bottom half of the diagram.

INTERNAL PROCESSER

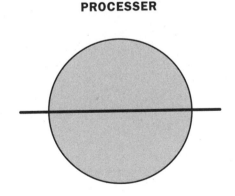

EXTERNAL PROCESSER

3. Next, think about the way you handle addressing an issue with this person. Are you more likely to talk or argue with them about the issue at hand or to just pretend you are fine?

- If you are more likely to address the issue, you are an external expresser and fall into the left side of the diagram below.

- If you are more likely to not address the issue and instead just pretend you are fine, you are an internal suppressor and fall into the right side of the diagram.

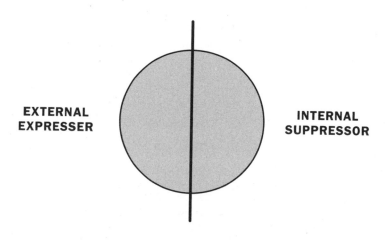

EXTERNAL
EXPRESSER

INTERNAL
SUPPRESSOR

4. Now that you've identified each of these determinants, you can see which quadrant you fall into in the diagram on the facing page and thus identify your reactor type with this particular relationship.

5. Now remember these important things:

- With different relationships, you will likely fall into different quadrants. So thinking about each of your important relationships, retake this assessment for each of them.

- We aren't using any of these labels as condemnations. They are simply gentle convictions that help us see the areas we need to work on. By implementing the strategies in this book, we can be well on our way to having healthier reactions—which means healthier relationships!

- If you are an expresser, there is a really good side to this— your honesty! (See the diagram.) Just remember to balance your honesty with the godly principle of peacemaking.

- If you are a suppressor, there is a really good side to this— your peacemaking ability. (See the diagram.) Just remember to balance your peacemaking with godly honesty.

- The goal of this exercise is "soul integrity," as indicated in the bull's-eye on the diagram. Soul integrity happens when we exhibit honesty that is also peaceable in each of our relationships.

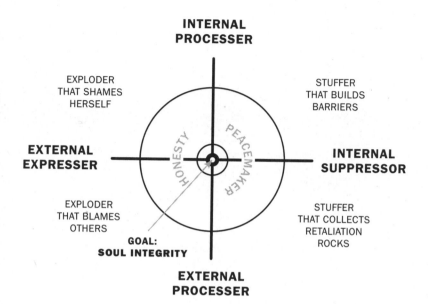

INTERNAL
PROCESSER

EXPLODER
THAT SHAMES
HERSELF

STUFFER
THAT BUILDS
BARRIERS

HONESTY

PEACEMAKER

EXTERNAL
EXPRESSER

INTERNAL
SUPPRESSOR

EXPLODER
THAT BLAMES
OTHERS

STUFFER
THAT COLLECTS
RETALIATION
ROCKS

GOAL:
SOUL INTEGRITY

EXTERNAL
PROCESSER

About Lysa TerKeurst

Lysa TerKeurst is a wife to Art and mom to five priority blessings named Jackson, Mark, Hope, Ashley, and Brooke. The author of more than a dozen books, including the *New York Times*-bestselling *Made to Crave*, she has been featured on *Focus on the Family*, *Good Morning America*, the *Oprah Winfrey Show*, and in *O Magazine*. Her greatest passion is inspiring women to say yes to God and take part in the awesome adventure He has designed every soul to live. While she is the cofounder of Proverbs 31 Ministries, to those who know her best she is simply a carpooling mom who loves her family, loves Jesus passionately, and struggles like the rest of us with laundry, junk drawers, and cellulite.

WEBSITE: If you enjoyed this book by Lysa, you'll love all the additional resources found at *www.Ungluedbook.com*, *www.LysaTerKeurst.com*, and *www.Proverbs31.org*.

BLOG: Dialog with Lysa through her daily blog, see pictures of her family, and follow her speaking schedule. She'd love to meet you at an event in your area!

www.LysaTerKeurst.com.

AM I TRYING TO PROVE THAT I'M RIGHT, OR IMPROVE THE RELATIONSHIP?

MY FEELINGS ARE INDICATORS, NOT DICTATORS.

THE ONE WHO HOLDS THE TONGUE, HOLDS THE POWER.

IF THIS IS THE WORST THING THAT HAPPENS TO ME TODAY, IT'S STILL A PRETTY GOOD DAY.

A GIFT JUST FOR YOU

Get these free colorful key tags to keep you inspired and on track. Place your order by emailing: resources@Proverbs31.org and reference "Unglued Key Tags" in the subject line. The only charge is $1 to cover shipping and handling. Bulk orders for Bible studies and small groups are also available with special shipping rates.

ABOUT PROVERBS 31 MINISTRIES

If you were inspired by the *Unglued Devotional* and desire to deepen your own personal relationship with Jesus Christ, I encourage you to connect with Proverbs 31 Ministries. Proverbs 31 Ministries exists to be a trusted friend who will take you by the hand and walk by your side, leading you one step closer to the heart of God, through:

· *ENCOURAGEMENT FOR TODAY,* FREE ONLINE DAILY DEVOTIONS

· THE *P31 WOMAN* MONTHLY MAGAZINE

· DAILY RADIO PROGRAMS

For more information about Proverbs 31 Ministries, visit: www.Proverbs31.org

To inquire about having Lysa speak at your event, email: info@lysaterkeurst.com

Unglued

Making Wise Choices in the Midst of Raw Emotions

Lysa TerKeurst,
New York Times *Bestselling Author*

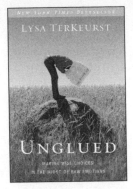

God gave us emotions to experience life, not destroy it! Lysa TerKeurst admits that she, like most women, has had experiences where others bump into her happy and she comes emotionally unglued. We stuff, we explode, or we react somewhere in between. What do we do with these raw emotions? Is it really possible to make emotions work for us instead of against us? Yes, and in her usual inspiring and practical way, Lysa will show you how. Filled with gut-honest personal examples and biblical teaching, *Unglued* will equip you to:

- Know with confidence how to resolve conflict in your important relationships.
- Find peace in your most difficult relationships as you learn to be honest but kind when offended.
- Identify what type of reactor you are and how to significantly improve your communication.
- Respond with no regrets by managing your tendencies to stuff or explode.
- Gain a deep sense of calm by responding to situations out of your control.

Available in stores and online!

Unglued Participant's Guide with DVD

Making Wise Choices in the Midst of Raw Emotions

Lysa TerKeurst

Experience the six-session video-based study (filmed in and around Florence, Italy) based on Lysa TerKeurst's bestselling book *Unglued*.

The participant's guide and DVD are sold separately or in a pack.

Sessions include:

SESSION 1: Grace for the Unglued

SESSION 2: Freedom for the Unglued

SESSION 3: Four Kinds of Unglued

SESSION 4: A Procedure Manual for the Unglued

SESSION 5: Lingering Words for the Unglued

SESSION 6: Imperfect Progress for the Unglued

Available in stores and online!

Made to Crave

Satisfying Your Deepest Desire with God, Not Food

Lysa TerKeurst,
New York Times *Bestselling Author*

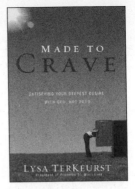

Made to Crave is the missing link between a woman's desire to be healthy and the spiritual empowerment necessary to make that happen. The reality is we were made to crave. Craving isn't a bad thing. But we must realize God created us to crave more of Him. Many of us have misplaced that craving by overindulging in physical pleasures instead of lasting spiritual satisfaction. If you are struggling with unhealthy eating habits, you can break the "I'll start again Monday" cycle, and start feeling good about yourself today. Learn to stop beating yourself up over the numbers on the scale. Discover that your weight loss struggle isn't a curse but rather a blessing in the making, and replace justifications that lead to diet failure with empowering go-to scripts that lead to victory. You can reach your healthy weight goal—and grow closer to God in the process.

Also Available:

Made to Crave Curriculum

Available in stores and online!

Made to Crave Action Plan Participant's Guide with DVD

Your Journey to Healthy Living

Lysa TerKeurst and Dr. Ski Chilton with Christine Anderson

According to *New York Times* bestselling author Lysa TerKeurst, craving isn't a bad thing, but we must realize God created us to crave so we'd ultimately desire more of Him in our lives. Many of us have misplaced that craving, over-indulging in physical pleasures instead of lasting spiritual satisfaction. *Made to Crave Action Plan*—a follow-up curriculum to *Made to Crave*—will help women implement a long-term plan of action for healthy living. In this six-session video-based study, women will be encouraged by Bible teaching from Lysa, uplifted by testimonies from women like Christian music chart-topper Mandisa, and empowered with healthy living tips from Dr. Ski Chilton, an expert in molecular medicine. This curriculum will help women who found their "want to" by participating in the *Made to Crave* study master the "how to" of living a healthy physical life as well as cultivate a rich and full relationship with God. *Made to Crave Action Plan* gives women of all ages biblical encouragement for both their physical and spiritual journeys plus healthy living tips for use in their everyday lives.

Sessions include:

1. **Take Action:** Identify Your First Steps
2. **Eat Smart:** Add Fish and Increase Fiber
3. **Embrace the Equation:** Exercise and Reduce Calories
4. **Maximize Key Nutrients:** Increase Nutrient-Rich Fruits and Veggies
5. **Practice the Five Principles:** Keep Working Your Plan
6. **Make a Courageous Choice:** Direct Your Heart to Love and Perseverance

Becoming More Than a Good Bible Study Girl

Lysa TerKeurst,
New York Times *Bestselling Author*

Is Something Missing in Your Life?

Lysa TerKeurst knows what it's like to consider God just another thing on her to-do list. For years she went through the motions of a Christian life: Go to church. Pray. Be nice.

Longing for a deeper connection between what she knew in her head and her everyday reality, she wanted to personally experience God's presence.

Drawing from her own remarkable story of step-by-step faith, Lysa invites you to uncover the spiritually exciting life we all yearn for. With her trademark wit and spiritual wisdom, Lysa will help you:

- Learn how to make a Bible passage come alive in your own devotion time.
- Replace doubt, regret, and envy with truth, confidence, and praise.
- Stop the unhealthy cycles of striving and truly learn to love who you are and what you've been given.
- Discover how to have inner peace and security in any situation.
- Sense God responding to your prayers.

The adventure God has in store for your life just might blow you away.

Also Available:

Becoming More Than a Good Bible Study Girl Curriculum